Ella Butcher

2025

Copyright © 2025 by Ella Butcher
Cover and Art Design by Ella Butcher.

All rights reserved. No part of this work may be reproduced or transmitted in any form or by any means, electronic or mechanical, including scanning, photocopying, or recording, without permission. Some of the Support Your Mental information is gathered from different sources for educational purposes and may not reflect the most current updates. The authors and publishers do not guarantee the accuracy of the information in this book.

For permission to use material from the book (other than for review purposes) or for more information, please contact us at www.peachesandcream.org

ISBN: 978-0-9834266-1-5

Printed in the United States of America.

Some of the people depicted in mock-ups are models, and such images are being used to display the Peaches and Cream Foundation products and for illustrative purposes only. Information may have changed since publication.

First Edition: 2025
Published by Ella Butcher
The Peaches and Cream Foundation
www.peachesandcream.org

The proceeds from this book will go to the
Peaches and Cream Foundation, which is a 501(c) (3) non-profit organization.

TABLE OF CONTENTS

- **4** Introduction
- **14** Understanding Mental Health
- **38** Building a Strong Foundation
- **45** Cultivating Positive Thinking Patterns
- **49** Managing Anxiety and Stress
- **54** Enhancing Emotional Intelligence
- **58** Building Resilience and Overcoming Challenges
- **63** Navigating Social Media and Digital Well-being
- **67** Youth Mental Health
- **102** Mental Wellness Challenge and Planner
- **108** Certificate of Participation Completion

INTRODUCTION

Welcome to "Support Your Mental" for Youth and Adults, this book is designed to help you understand and improve your mental health: by providing valuable insights, tools, examples, and exercises that support your journey toward a healthier mind. We have included a colorful-dot design throughout the book for your enjoyment and engagement. We hope the dots make you happy as you read. **"The formatting may vary across different formats, as it is designed for accessibility. This book is available in paperback, eBook, and audiobook formats, ensuring that people who struggle with small print can access it."**

Mental health is a vital component of our overall well-being. It affects how we think, feel, and act in different situations. It also influences our relationships, our productivity, and our happiness. However, many people struggle with mental health issues at some point in their lives. These issues can range from stress, anxiety, and depression to more serious conditions such as bipolar disorder, schizophrenia, and post-traumatic stress disorder. Some of these issues may be caused by biological factors, such as genetics or brain chemistry, while others may be triggered by environmental factors, such as trauma, abuse, or social isolation.

- The **first step** is to recognize that you are not alone and that you deserve to feel better.

- The **second step** is to seek professional help if you need it. There is no shame in asking for help when you are struggling with your mental health.

- The **third step** is to take action to improve your mental health. This may be, like eating healthier, exercising more, sleeping better, or reducing substance use. It may also involve learning some coping skills, such as mindfulness, and relaxation techniques.

We hope that this book will inspire you to take charge of your mental health and pursue your goals with confidence and optimism. We wish you all the best in your quest for a healthier mind.

ELLA BUTCHER'S STORY

As the founder of the Peaches and Cream Foundation, I was compelled to write this book due to my profound mental struggles. My upbringing in the South, where prayer was the answer to everything, left many families oblivious to their mental health issues, which eventually pushed me to a breaking point. Over two decades, I dedicated my life to aiding people and children, leading to the establishment of the Peaches and Cream Foundation in 2004. My journey was marked by an unwavering commitment to helping less fortunate youth, all without relying on government funding. The Peaches and Cream Foundation operates as a 501(c) (3) non-profit organization, and our enduring mission is to make a meaningful impact, a mission we continue to pursue with strength and resilience. We were continuing on the next page.

My personal journey took an extraordinary turn several years ago, battling my mental health issues, which included anxiety disorders and Trichotillomania, a compulsive hair-pulling condition. These challenges had haunted me since childhood, yet I remained oblivious to their underlying causes. I often sought solitude, avoiding crowded places and social activities, attributing it to having "bad nerves." It wasn't until I sought the help of a therapist that I discovered I shared a background with many others.

This revelation inspired me to believe that, once I had my own life together, I could extend a helping hand to other women and children who silently grapple with mental challenges. They often felt ashamed to seek help, lacked support, or faced cultural stigma, particularly women like me who embraced the term "successful mess." Meaning, I was doing great things, but I didn't know I was a mess.

I wholeheartedly believe that the challenges I've endured, and still face, are not something I'd wish upon anyone. Mental health is a genuine issue that does not discriminate. Unless you've personally experienced it, you may not fully grasp its impact. This book aims to shed light on my journey through mental illness and how it led me to create a mental wellness initiative and embark on a mental wellness movement.

Many individuals claim they want to help the community, but often exploit every opportunity for financial gain, rather than addressing the root issues. The Peaches and Cream Foundation is different. Our goal is to make a difference through our mental health initiative, with a mission to assist as many youths as possible.

The unexpectedly tragic loss of our vice chair seven years ago on Thanksgiving Day, attributed to mental health issues, further intensified my determination to bring about positive change. I realized the urgent need to support youth and college students, who often bear the heavy burden of mental illness and the specter of suicide. The Peaches and Cream Foundation remains steadfast in its dedication to empowering children's mental health and eradicating the stigma surrounding these crucial issues. If you'd like to join our cause and get involved with our mental health initiatives, please visit our website at **www.peachesandcream.org.** Enjoy the Ride!

Testimonial

As someone deeply passionate about content creation in the fields of psychology and mental health, I couldn't have asked for a more fulfilling role than being able to contribute to the "Support Your Mental" book, written to offer support to young people dealing with mental health issues. Hence, I would like to deeply thank Ms. Butcher and the Peaches and Cream Foundation for allowing me to play an integral role in bringing this book to life!

Children and young teens face complex mental health challenges and need more resources, support, and guidance. I used to struggle with mental health too, and I know how important it is to educate and raise awareness about it. My mental health struggles have made me more empathetic and stronger, and I want to use them to advocate for others. I think mental health education and sharing our stories can reduce stigma and empower us to improve our mental well-being.

The Peaches and Cream Foundation is a unique organization. Ms. Butcher is devoted to helping underprivileged young girls and changing their lives. I am privileged and grateful to work as her assistant and learn from her.

Ms. Butcher has been a wonderful mentor to me, helping me improve my skills and overcome my challenges. My internship at the foundation has been a priceless learning opportunity, giving me practical skills that benefit both my career and my service to the youth with mental health needs. As the Psych Ambassador for the foundation, I look forward to more projects that create positive impacts for youth worldwide.

The "Support Your Mental" book is a result of Ms. Butcher and the interns' dedication to helping those who need it. I've learned that this book is more than a book; it's a priceless resource that can transform your mental health if you follow its guidance. I hope this book helps you in your mental health journey and gives you the power to change your mind for the better.

"Ashlynn" Myat Thiri Pyae
Former Psychology Ambassador & Intern

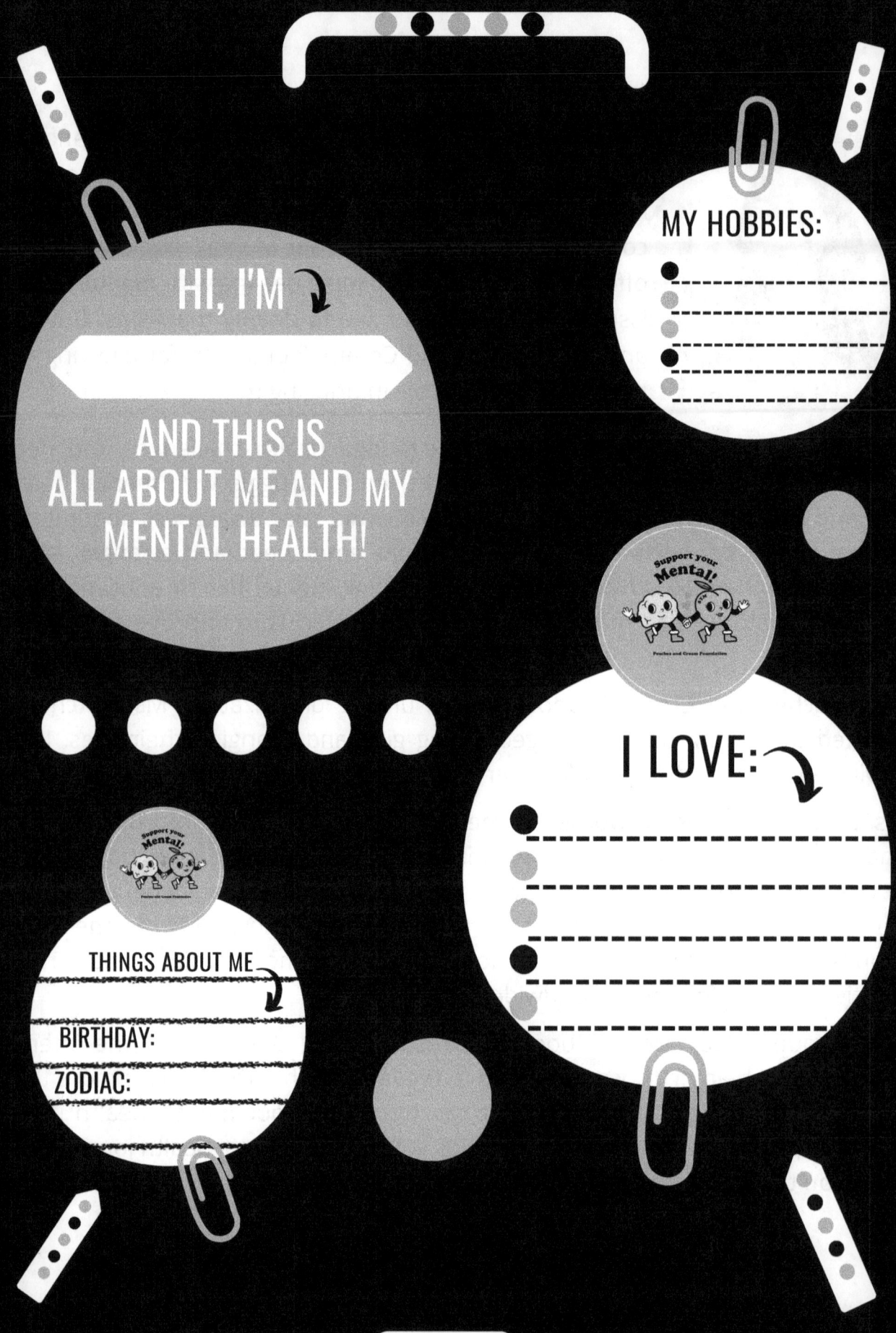

SUPPORT YOUR MENTAL ROLL CALL!

HOW DO YOU NORMALLY FEEL?

DATE _____

HOW DO YOU NORMALLY FEEL?

EXPRESS HOW YOU FEEL TODAY.

SAD | OK | ALONE | HAPPY

DEPRESSED | GIVING UP

HOW CAN YOU BOOST YOUR MENTAL HEALTH?

WHAT WERE THREE THINGS ON YOUR MIND THIS WEEK?
- _____
- _____
- _____

WHAT DO YOU FEEL GOOD ABOUT RIGHT NOW?

THINGS THAT TRIGGER NEGATIVE EMOTIONS
- _____
- _____
- _____
- _____

RANK YOUR MENTAL HEALTH THIS WEEK

☆ ☆ ☆ ☆ ☆

I'M YOUR MENTAL WELLNESS GUIDE

To enhance your learning experience, we have also prepared helpful items that you can purchase from our website at www.peachesandcream.org under the Shop tab.

These items are:

- **Customized T-shirt:** Design a T-shirt with a positive message or an uplifting quote. Wearing a shirt with a positive affirmation can boost your mood and serve as a reminder of self-care and self-love.

- **Inspirational Poster:** Create a motivational poster with a beautiful design and an inspiring quote. Hang it on your wall as a visual reminder of your strength and resilience.

- **Mindfulness Meditation Cushion (Which is a Pillow):** Print a design on a meditation cushion to enhance your meditation practice. The cushion provides comfort and support while you focus on mindfulness and relaxation.

- **Customized Water Bottle:** Customize a water bottle with a positive affirmation or a calming design. Staying hydrated is essential for your overall well-being; having a personalized bottle can make it more enjoyable.

- **Support Your Mental Bag:** Include a small bag or pouch that can be used as a "SYM bag." This can be a place to store notes or small items representing your wishes or goals. It serves as a reminder to focus on your aspirations and provides a tangible way to keep them close.

- **Gratitude Journal:** Design a journal with prompts for gratitude practice. It will encourage you to focus on the positive aspects of your life and foster a sense of appreciation.

- **Mental Health Awareness Stickers:** Design stickers with mental health awareness messages and distribute them to raise awareness and reduce stigma. You can use them on notebooks, laptops, or even share them with others.

- **Bookmarks:** Design custom bookmarks with uplifting quotes or coping techniques. Bookmarks can be used during reading sessions as a way to mark your progress and serve as a gentle reminder of self-care and relaxation.

- **Coffee Mug:** Customize a coffee mug with a positive message or an inspiring design. Having a favorite mug for your warm beverages can bring comfort and relaxation during moments of self-reflection or as part of your morning routine.

- **Pin Button:** Create a pin button or badge with a motivational phrase or an image that resonates with you. You can wear it on clothing or attach it to bags as a symbol of strength and resilience. You can also mix and match different items to create a personalized bundle.

In addition to these items, we also recommend that you purchase the "Support Your Mental" workbook and planner that accompany this book at www.amazon.com. The workbook contains exercises and activities that will help you apply what you learn in the book and enhance your mental health knowledge. The workbook is an important part of the book, as it will help you reinforce your learning and track your progress.

We hope that you enjoy this book and the items that we offer. We believe that by supporting your mental health and well-being, you can live a happier and more fulfilling life. Thank you for choosing us as your partner in this journey.

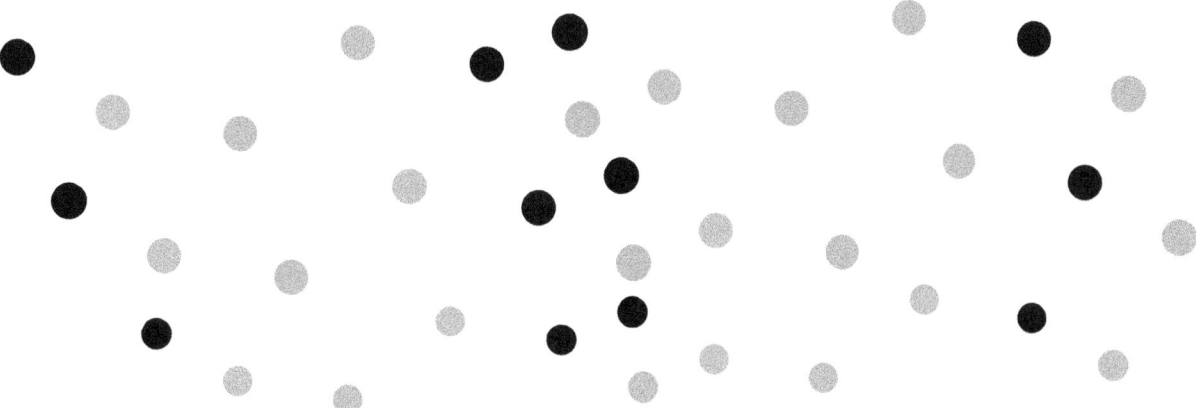

DISCLAIMER:

THIS BOOK AIMS TO SHARE GENERAL INFORMATION AND EDUCATIONAL INSIGHTS ON MENTAL HEALTH TOPICS, BASED ON VARIOUS SOURCES SUCH AS THE WEB AND PERSONAL EXPERIENCES. **<u>IT IS NOT MEANT TO REPLACE PROFESSIONAL MEDICAL ADVICE, DIAGNOSIS, OR TREATMENT</u>**. IF YOU OR SOMEONE YOU CARE ABOUT IS STRUGGLING WITH MENTAL HEALTH ISSUES, PLEASE GET IN TOUCH WITH A QUALIFIED HEALTHCARE PROVIDER.

SOME MOCKUPS IN THIS BOOK ARE NOT ENDORSEMENTS OF THE PEACHES AND CREAM FOUNDATION OR ITS AFFILIATES. THEY ARE ONLY FOR ILLUSTRATION PURPOSES AND TO SHOW OUR MERCHANDISE. THE PEACHES AND CREAM FOUNDATION DOES NOT GET ANY BENEFIT FROM SOME OF THE INFORMATION SHOWN IN THE BOOK.

VISITING WEBSITES LISTED IN THIS BOOK, ELLA BUTCHER AND THE PEACHES AND CREAM FOUNDATION DO NOT GUARANTEE THE RELIABILITY OF ANY OTHER WEBSITES. THE PEACHES AND CREAM FOUNDATION (PNCF) AND ITS AFFILIATES DO NOT ENDORSE OR SUPPORT THIRD PARTIES, INFORMATION, OR PRODUCTS OFFERED ON THE WEBSITES YOU VISIT. PLEASE ENSURE THAT YOU FOLLOW THE PRIVACY POLICY OF THE WEBSITES YOU VISIT.

In these sections, you will explore what mental health means and why it matters for everyone. We will also discuss some of the common mental health disorders and challenges that youth and adults may face. You will learn how to recognize the signs and symptoms of these issues and how to seek help when needed.

Finally, we will address the stigma that often surrounds mental health and how to overcome it with compassion and understanding.

Have a seat and relax!

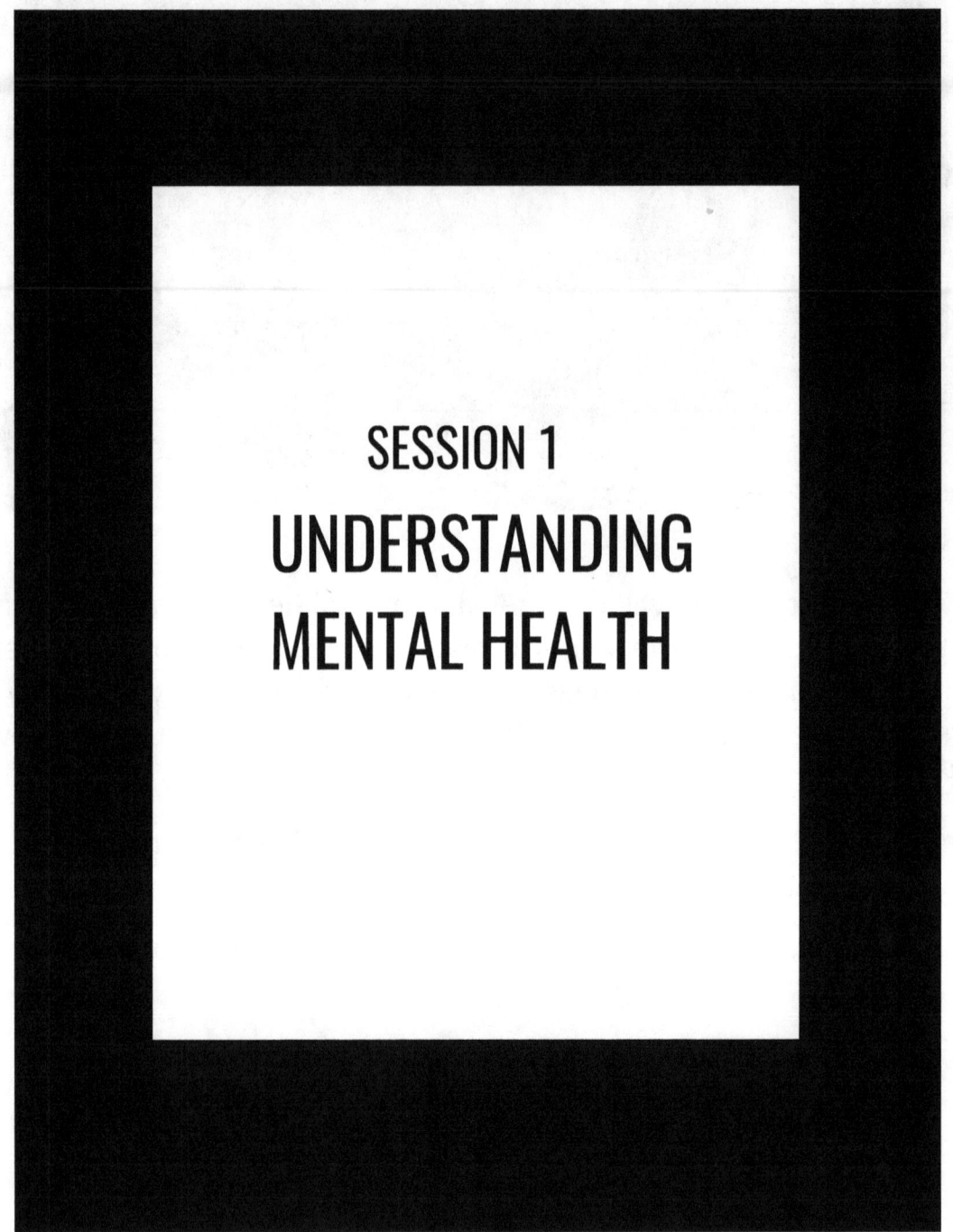

SESSION 1
UNDERSTANDING MENTAL HEALTH

UNDERSTANDING MENTAL HEALTH

"1 in 4 people, will experience a mental health problem."

Mental health is a vital aspect of our well-being that affects how we think, feel, and act. It also influences our ability to cope with stress, relate to others, and make decisions.

Mental health is the state of well-being that encompasses our cognitive, affective, and social domains. It influences how we perceive, process, and respond to environmental stimuli.

Optimal mental health enables us to adapt to changes, manage stress, and thrive daily. Mental health issues, however, can impair our functioning, causing emotional turmoil, interpersonal conflicts, and physical ailments. Mental health challenges are common and can affect anyone, regardless of age, gender, culture, or background.

In the United States, 22.8% of adults (approximately 57.8 million people) experienced mental illness in 2021, representing 1 in 5 adults.

Globally, nearly one billion people suffer from some form of mental disorder, including approximately one in seven teenagers. These figures underscore the critical importance of mental health support and awareness worldwide.

Please keep in mind that this list is not exhaustive, and there are many other mental health disorders with distinct symptoms. Some of the most common mental health challenges faced by youth and adults include:

1. Anxiety disorders: These are a group of mental health conditions that cause excessive fear and worry that interfere with different aspects of life, such as school, work, or relationships. They can also cause physical symptoms, such as restlessness, fatigue, muscle tension, or insomnia. There are several types of anxiety disorders:

a) Generalized anxiety disorder (GAD): People feel anxious and nervous most of the time, even when there is no specific reason to be. They may worry about various aspects of life, such as health, work, family, or money. They may also have physical symptoms, such as restlessness, fatigue, muscle tension, or insomnia.

b) Separation anxiety disorder: People have a fear of being separated from someone they are attached to, such as a parent, spouse, or child. They may worry excessively about losing or harming their loved one or being abandoned by them. They may have difficulty leaving their home or being alone. <u>They may also experience nausea, headaches, or nightmares</u>.

c) Social anxiety disorder (SAD): People have a fear of being judged, rejected, or embarrassed in social or performance situations. They may feel self-conscious, nervous, or ashamed around other people. They may avoid social situations or activities that involve interacting with others, such as speaking in public, dating, or eating in front of others.

d) Panic disorder: People have sudden and repeated attacks of intense fear and discomfort, called panic attacks. During a panic attack, they may experience chest pain, shortness of breath, trembling, sweating, or dizziness. They may also fear losing control, going crazy, or dying. <u>They may avoid places or situations that trigger their panic attacks</u>.

e) Phobias: A phobia is an excessive and irrational fear reaction to a specific object, situation, or feeling. People with phobias often experience intense anxiety and panic when they encounter or think about their fear. <u>Phobias can interfere with daily life and cause significant distress</u>.

"It is okay to have phobias if you are unaware of them, but once you are aware of them, you should not let them control you. You should take action to overcome them. I was in the same situation before. I had them, but I did not know it." - Ella Butcher

There are three main categories of phobias: social phobia, agoraphobia, and specific phobia.

- Social phobia is a fear of social situations where a person might be judged or embarrassed. People with social phobia may avoid speaking in public, meeting new people, or eating in front of others.

- Agoraphobia is a fear of being in places where escape is difficult, or help is not available. People with agoraphobia may avoid crowded places, public transportation, or leaving their homes.

- Specific phobia is a fear of a specific object or situation, such as spiders, heights, or flying. People with a specific phobia may go to great lengths to avoid their fear object.

Phobias can cause symptoms such as nausea, trembling, rapid heartbeat, and feelings of unreality. Phobias can be treated with psychotherapy, medication, or exposure therapy.

According to the World Health Organization, anxiety **disorders are very common throughout the world and in the US.**

Anxiety disorders can affect people of any age, but they are more common in women than in men.

- They affect about 264 million people globally and 40 million adults in the US.
- They affect around 58 million children globally, and about 5.8 million or 9.4% of **children aged 3-17 years** in the US.

Anxiety disorders can affect children in school in many ways. For example:

- A child with **social anxiety** may have an intense fear of being judged by others, which can make it difficult for them to participate in class, make friends, or join extracurricular activities.
- A child with **separation anxiety** may have a hard time leaving their parents or caregivers, which can cause them to miss school or have tantrums at drop-off.
- A child with **generalized anxiety** may worry excessively about their school performance, homework, tests, or future, which can interfere with their concentration, motivation, or sleep.
- A child with **panic disorder** may have sudden episodes of intense fear that cause physical symptoms like a racing heart, sweating, shaking, or trouble breathing, which can be very scary and disruptive for them and others around them.

Anxiety disorders can be treated with medication, therapy, coaching, and strategies that suit the person's individual needs and strengths.

> You can be brave, you can be strong, and you are not alone. Anxiety may make you feel scared, but you can face your fears and overcome them. You have the power to calm your mind and body, and to find peace and happiness. You are loved, you are valued, you are important.

More information about mental disorders can be found at: www.nimh.nih.gov.

2. Mood disorders:

These are characterized by persistent or recurrent changes in mood that affect how a person feels, thinks, and behaves. Mood disorders can cause symptoms such as depression, bipolar disorder, dysthymia, and cyclothymia.

3. Psychotic disorders:

These are characterized by distorted perceptions of reality that affect how a person thinks, feels, and behaves. Psychotic disorders can cause symptoms such as hallucinations, delusions, paranoia, and schizophrenia.

4 . Eating disorders:

These are characterized by abnormal or unhealthy eating habits that affect a person's physical and mental health. Eating disorders can cause symptoms such as anorexia nervosa, bulimia nervosa, binge eating disorder, and avoidant/restrictive food intake disorder.

5. Substance use disorders:

These are characterized by the misuse or dependence on alcohol, drugs, or other substances that affect a person's physical and mental health. Substance use disorders can cause symptoms such as withdrawal, tolerance, cravings, impaired judgment, and addiction.

> *"Mental disorders are not personal failures they are challenges that can be improved when identifying and knowing you have them, with, help, courage, and desire to get help."*

6. Personality disorders:

These are characterized by enduring patterns of thinking, feeling, and behaving that deviate from the norms of one's culture and cause distress or impairment in social, occupational, or other areas of functioning. Personality disorders can cause symptoms such as antisocial personality disorder, borderline personality disorder, narcissistic personality disorder, and avoidant personality disorder.

The Link Between Depression and Other Mental Disorders:

Depression is a common mental disorder that affects how a person feels, thinks, and behaves. It can cause persistent feelings of sadness and loss of interest. It can also cause physical problems and make it hard to do normal things.

Depression is not a disease, but a disorder. A disease is a physical condition with a specific cause, such as a virus or bacteria. A disorder is a mental or behavioral pattern that causes distress or impairment, or involves changes in the brain's chemistry or structure, but may not have a clear cause. Depression is a disorder because it involves changes in the brain's chemistry and structure, and the exact causes of depression are not fully known.

Depression can be hard to recognize because it can manifest in different ways for different people and can also develop gradually, without a person realizing that depressive thoughts and feelings are increasingly dominating their perspective and their life. Depression can be triggered by genetic, biological, environmental, and psychological factors, and can occur at any age and in any gender. Depression is treatable, and there are effective therapies for mild, moderate, and severe depression. Some factors can increase the risk.

- **Risk factors: Some things that can increase the chance of getting depression are:**
    - Having family members with depression
    - Going through a lot of stress or trauma and feeling lonely or isolated
    - Having a chronic illness or pain, using drugs or alcohol
    - Using drugs or alcohol

- **Diagnosis and treatment: People who have depression can get help from doctors or therapists, who can:**
    - Check their symptoms and medical history
    - Prescribe medicine to balance their mood
    - Provide counseling or therapy to talk about their problems

- **Symptoms: Some signs that someone may have depression are:**

    - Feeling worthless, guilty, or hopeless
    - Losing interest in things they used to enjoy
    - Having trouble sleeping, eating, or focusing
    - Thinking about death or suicide
    - Feeling physical pain or tiredness

- **Types: There are different kinds of depression, such as:**

    - Major depressive disorder (MDD): A severe form of depression that lasts for at least two weeks and affects most aspects of life.
    - Persistent depressive disorder (PDD): A mild but chronic form of depression that lasts for at least two years.
    - Postpartum depression (PPD): A type of depression that affects some women after giving birth.
    - Seasonal affective disorder (SAD): A type of depression that occurs during the winter months when there is less sunlight.
    - Bipolar disorder: A condition that causes alternating episodes of depression and mania (a state of high energy and mood).

- **Statistics: Some facts and numbers about depression are:**

    - In 2020, about 14.8 million U.S. adults had a major depressive episode that made it hard to function.
    - Depression affects more than 280 million people of all ages around the world (about 3.5% of the global population).
    - Depression is the main cause of disability worldwide, as measured by how many years people live with it.
    - In 2019, about 39% of adults with major depression did not get any treatment.
    - About 4.1 million teens aged 12 to 17 in the U.S. had a major depressive episode.
    - More than 1 in 20 children aged 6 to 17 in the U.S., in 2011-2012, had anxiety or depression according to their parents.

7. Attention-Deficit/Hyperactivity Disorder (ADHD)

ADHD is a condition that affects the brain's attention, thinking, behavior, and impulse control. It reduces brain chemicals like dopamine and norepinephrine that help with focus and alertness. People with ADHD may struggle with distractions, organization, paying attention, time management, task completion, or following directions. They may also be very active, restless, talkative, or impulsive. These symptoms can interfere with different aspects of life, such as school, work, or relationships. People with ADHD can enhance their focus with medication, therapy, coaching, and strategies that suit their needs and strengths.

Attention-deficit disorder (ADD) andattention-deficit/hyperactivity disorder (ADHD) are indeed the same condition; it's just that ADHD has had several name changes in the last three decades. This is because, as more research is carried out, understanding grows, and the name has been changed to reflect that knowledge. **ADD** was an older term used to describe a specific type of ADHD.

Diagnosis Criteria

- For children up to age 16 years: Six or more symptoms of inattention must be present.
- For adolescents aged 17 years and older, as well as adults, five or more symptoms of inattention are required.
- These symptoms should persist for at least 6 months and significantly interfere with daily functioning.

Who can diagnose or treat ADHD?

- Mental health professionals, such as psychologists or psychiatrists, can diagnose ADHD.
- Primary care providers, like pediatricians, can also make the diagnosis.
- Healthcare providers typically gather information from parents, teachers, and other adults who interact with the individual in various settings (home, school, peers).
- Family health history is important in understanding attention and learning problems.

There are three types of ADHD:

Inattentive type, Hyperactive-impulsive type, and Combined type. Each type has different symptoms and may require different treatment approaches. Here is a brief overview of each type:

Inattentive type:

- People with this type of ADHD have trouble paying attention to details, staying focused on tasks, listening to others, following instructions, or organizing their work. They may also be easily distracted by irrelevant stimuli or forgetful in daily activities. They do not show significant signs of hyperactivity or impulsivity.

Hyperactive-impulsive type:

- People with this type of ADHD have difficulty sitting still, controlling their impulses, or waiting for their turn. They may also be very active, talkative, or impatient. They may act without thinking or interrupt others. They do not show significant signs of inattention.

Combined type:

- People with this type of ADHD have symptoms of both inattention and hyperactivity-impulsivity. They may have trouble focusing, staying on task, following rules, or controlling their emotions. They may also be restless, fidgety, noisy, or impulsive.

The number of children who suffer from ADHD in the world and the US:

- Worldwide: An estimated 129 million children and adolescents between the ages of 5 to 19 years have ADHD.
- US: The estimated number of children aged 3–17 years ever diagnosed with ADHD, according to a national survey of parents, is 6 million (9.8%) using data from 2016-2019. This number includes:

    > 3–5 years: 265,000 (2%)
    > 6–11 years: 2.4 million (10%)
    > 12–17 years: 3.3 million (13%)

The worldwide prevalence of adult ADHD is estimated at 2.5%.

- The U.S. lifetime prevalence of ADHD in adults aged 18 to 44 years is estimated to be 8.1%, with the current prevalence estimated to be 4.4%.
- About 5.4% of men in the U.S. have been diagnosed with ADHD, while 3.2% of women in the U.S. have the same.
- ADHD is among the most common mental disorders in children and teens, but plenty of adults have it too. It's estimated that adult ADHD affects more than 8 million adults (or up to 5% of Americans).

The exact cause of ADHD is not clear, but there are several factors that may contribute to it. Some of the possible causes of ADHD are:

- **Brain anatomy and function:** Some studies have shown that people with ADHD have differences in the structure and activity of certain brain regions, especially those that control attention and activity levels.
- Genes and heredity: ADHD tends to run in families, and research suggests that genes play a role in the development of the disorder. **A child with ADHD has a 25% chance of having a parent with ADHD.**
- **Environmental factors:** Some environmental factors, such as exposure to lead, tobacco, alcohol, or other toxins during pregnancy or childhood, may increase the risk of developing ADHD.
- **Developmental problems:** Some problems with the central nervous system during critical periods of development may also affect the risk of ADHD.

If you would like to learn more about ADHD, you can check out the link: https://www.cdc.gov.

Notes:

_____
_____
_____
_____
_____

8. Obsessive-Compulsive Disorder: This is a chronic anxiety disorder where a person experiences unreasonable, uncontrollable, or recurring thoughts followed by a behavioral response. People with OCD may have either obsessions or compulsions, or both, and these can interfere with a person's daily life and cause distress.

Common symptoms of OCD are:

- **Obsessions:** These are repeated, unwanted, and intrusive thoughts, images, or impulses that cause anxiety or distress. Some examples of obsessions are fear of contamination, doubt, need for order, aggressive or violent thoughts, or sexual or religious thoughts.

- **Compulsions:** These are repetitive behaviors or mental acts that a person feels driven to perform to reduce the anxiety caused by obsessions. Some examples of compulsions are washing, checking, counting, praying, or arranging.

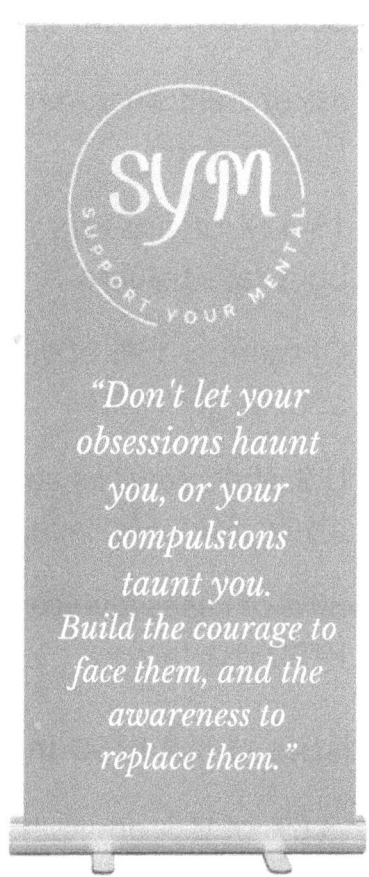

OCD statistics:

- OCD statistics show that 2.3% of the population has OCD, or 1 in 40 adults and 1 in 100 children in the U.S.

- OCD is more common in females (1.8%) than in males (0.5%) in a 12-month period.

- Nearly two-thirds of people with OCD had major symptoms before age 25.

- OCD can affect a person's life due to intrusive thoughts, anxiety, and uncertainty.

9. Post-Traumatic Stress Disorder (PTSD): PTSD is a mental health condition that can develop after experiencing or witnessing a traumatic event, such as abuse, violence, disaster, or death. PTSD can cause persistent, frightening thoughts and memories of the event, sleep problems, nightmares, detachment, or being easily startled.

Statistics about PTSD in children:

- 4% of children under 18 get PTSD from trauma
- 15-43% of girls and 14-43% of boys face trauma
- Of them, 3-15% of girls and 1-6% of boys get PTSD
- U.S. child services get 3M reports a year for 5.5M children
- 30% of cases involve abuse, a PTSD risk factor

Statistics about PTSD in adults:

- 3.6% of U.S. adults had PTSD last year, 6.8% in lifetime
- More females (5.2%) than males (1.8%) had PTSD
- 5% of U.S. adults have PTSD yearly, 13M in 2020

"It is possible to overcome PTSD, it does not have to last forever. You can heal from your trauma and take control of your life with help and support. Don't let the past dictate your future, make your future your past. Keep moving forward and excel."

If you or someone you know is struggling with PTSD, you can find more information and resources on the National Center for PTSD website: **www.ptsd.va.gov**. You can also call the National Suicide Prevention Lifeline at 1-800-273-8255 or text HOME to 74174.

10. Schizophrenia Spectrum Disorders: Schizophrenia spectrum disorders are a group of mental health conditions that affect a person's perception of reality, thinking, speech, emotions, and behavior. They are characterized by psychotic symptoms, such as hallucinations and delusions, as well as negative symptoms, such as social withdrawal and cognitive impairment.

The four main types of Schizophrenia Spectrum Disorders are:

a) Schizophrenia: The most common and severe form of psychosis, which requires at least two of the following symptoms for at least six months: hallucinations, delusions, disorganized speech, disorganized or catatonic behavior, or negative symptoms.

b) Schizophreniform disorder: A condition that has the same symptoms as schizophrenia but lasts for less than six months. Some people with this disorder may recover completely, while others may develop schizophrenia or schizoaffective disorder.

c) Schizoaffective disorder:
A condition that combines psychotic symptoms with mood disturbances, such as depression or bipolar disorder. The symptoms must occur independently of the mood episodes to distinguish this disorder from mood disorders with psychotic features.

d) Schizotypal personality disorder: A personality disorder that involves eccentric behavior, odd beliefs, and social anxiety. People with this disorder may experience mild forms of hallucinations or delusions, but they are aware that they are not real.

> *"Most people with schizophrenia make a recovery, although many will experience the occasional return of symptoms (relapses.)"*

Schizophrenia is a complex mental disorder that affects how a person thinks, feels, and behaves. The exact causes of schizophrenia are not fully understood, but researchers believe that a combination of factors may contribute to its development. **Some of these factors are:**

Genetics: Schizophrenia tends to run in families, but genes are not enough to cause it. Not all people with schizophrenia genes will get the disorder. This suggests that genes are not the only factor involved.

Environment: Schizophrenia can be triggered or worsened by environmental factors in people with a genetic risk. These factors may include infections, toxins, or stress before or after birth; birth problems; trauma; drugs; or loneliness.

The total number of people with schizophrenia in the world is estimated to be between **"48 million and 180 million"**. This is based on the global prevalence range of "0.25% to 0.75%" and the world population of about "7.9 billion" as of 2023.

Children: Schizophrenia spectrum disorders usually start in the mid-to-late 20s, but they can also start earlier, before the age of 18. This is called early-onset schizophrenia. The onset of schizophrenia in children younger than age 13 is extremely rare, and it is called childhood-onset schizophrenia.

> *Most people with schizophrenia are harmless to others. They're more likely to hurt themselves than anybody else. Sometimes that includes trying to take their own life. You should take any suicidal talk seriously, and pay attention to poems, notes, or any other things your loved one creates that are about death.*

However, this number may vary depending on the methods and criteria used to diagnose schizophrenia, as well as the availability and accessibility of mental health services in different regions.

If you would like to know more about schizophrenia, you can also check out these sources:

- NIMH: https://www.nimh.nih.gov/health/statistics/schizophrenia.
- World Health Organization (WHO). https://www.who.int/news-room/fact-sheets/detail/schizophrenia.

"Stigma hurts, understanding helps."

Mental health is essential for our well-being, but many people ignore or misjudge it. False beliefs and prejudices about mental health can stop people from getting help, support, or empathy. These negative views can stigmatize mental health and harm individuals and society.

Stigma involves:

- Labeling, stereotyping, discriminating, or excluding a group based on a certain attribute.
- In mental health, stigma can manifest as prejudice, fear, ignorance, or shame.

Stigma can cause negative consequences, such as:

- Reluctance to disclose mental health issues.
- Discouragement from accessing mental health services or following treatment plans.
- Poorer outcomes and lower quality of life.
- Social isolation, discrimination, harassment, or violence.

Stigma can also affect:

- Mental health affects self-esteem, confidence, and identity.

Stigma affects various aspects of life, such as:

- Personal relationships, education, employment, and social inclusion.

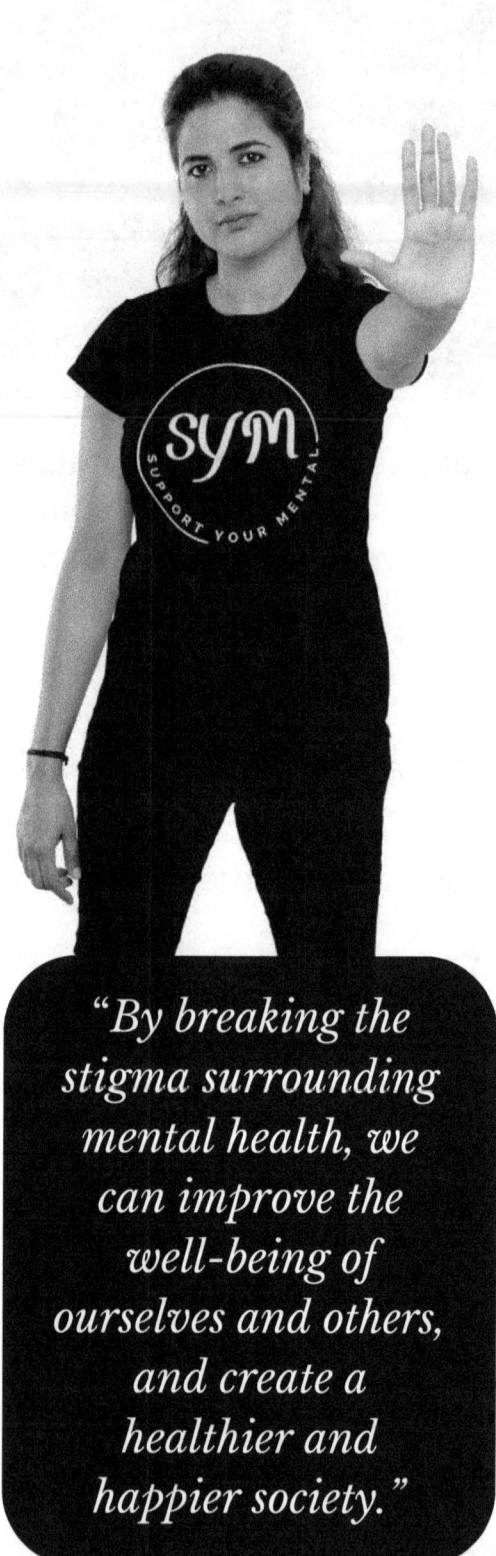

"By breaking the stigma surrounding mental health, we can improve the well-being of ourselves and others, and create a healthier and happier society."

Breaking the Stigma surrounding mental health is a collective responsibility that requires awareness, education, and action from all sectors of society. We can all play a role in challenging the myths and stereotypes that fuel stigma and creating a more supportive and inclusive environment for people with mental health problems.

We can do this by:

- Learning more about mental health and the factors that affect it.
- Recognizing and addressing our own biases and assumptions.
- Listening to and respecting the experiences and perspectives of people with mental health problems.
- Peaking up and speaking out against stigma and discrimination.
- Offering help and support to people who need it
- Seeking help and support when we need it.

Mental health conditions can have various causes, such as genetic factors, environmental factors, traumatic events, stressors, or medical conditions. They can also have various consequences, such as impaired functioning, reduced quality of life, increased risk of physical illness or injury, social isolation, stigma, discrimination, or suicide.

There are various types of treatments available for mental health challenges, such as psychotherapy, medication, self-help strategies, or support groups. With appropriate treatment and support, many people with mental health challenges can recover or manage their conditions effectively.

Therefore, it is important to seek help from a qualified mental health professional if one experiences any signs or symptoms of a mental health condition.

Notes:

_____
_____
_____
_____
_____
_____

Personalized Mental Health Treatment Through Pharmacogenomics:

In recent years, advancements in pharmacogenomics have revolutionized mental health treatment, offering a personalized approach to medication selection based on an individual's genetic makeup. Understanding the role of pharmacogenomics can have a significant impact on mental health diagnoses and treatment plans, according to licensed pharmacists.

Importance of Pharmacogenomics in Mental Health:

Pharmacogenomics examines how an individual's genetic variations influence their response to medications. In the realm of mental health, this translates to tailoring treatment plans to maximize efficacy and minimize potential side effects. By analyzing specific genes involved in drug metabolism, clinicians can identify which medications are likely to be most effective for a particular individual.

The Pharmacogenomics Process:

Obtaining DNA Testing for Medication Compatibility:

Individuals can undergo DNA testing to unveil insights into their genetic predispositions. This non-invasive process typically involves a simple cheek swab or saliva sample. The collected sample is then analyzed to identify variations in genes related to drug metabolism. Armed with this information, healthcare providers can make informed decisions about prescribing medications that align with the individual's genetic profile.

Preventing Trial-and-Error Approaches:

One of the most significant benefits of pharmacogenomic testing is its potential to spare individuals from the frustrating and often disheartening trial-and-error approach to finding the right medication. By pinpointing suitable options based on genetics, patients can avoid a prolonged journey of experimentation with various medications, reducing the risk of adverse reactions and hastening the path to effective treatment. Additionally, tailoring drug prescriptions based on genetic information can lead to more effective treatment, reducing the likelihood of side effects and unnecessary medical expenses."

Educational Proposition: Empowering Individuals with Knowledge:

The integration of pharmacogenomics into mental health education empowers individuals to actively participate in their treatment plans. Armed with a deeper understanding of how their genetic makeup influences medication responses, patients can engage in informed discussions with healthcare providers. This collaborative approach enhances communication, fosters trust, and ultimately contributes to more effective mental health care.

In conclusion, the integration of pharmacogenomics into mental health practices represents a pivotal shift toward personalized treatment plans. With the guidance of health professionals, individuals can navigate a more targeted and efficient path to mental well-being, minimizing the burden of trial and error and unlocking a new era of personalized mental health care.

Personalized Mental Health Treatment Through Pharmacogenomics- A Collaborative Approach:

In the realm of mental health, some individuals may find it challenging to articulate their genetic information to their healthcare providers. However, collaboration between patients, licensed pharmacists, and healthcare providers can bridge this gap.

The Pharmacist's Vital Role in Patient Advocacy:

Licensed pharmacists, with their expertise in medications and understanding of pharmacogenomics, emphasize the importance of this collaborative approach. Patients who may struggle to communicate their genetic information to their doctors can benefit from the seamless transmission of data facilitated by their pharmacist.

Faxing Information for Enhanced Communication:

To streamline this process, pharmacists can fax the relevant pharmacogenomic information directly to the patient's healthcare provider. This ensures that the critical genetic insights are seamlessly integrated into the patient's medical records, enabling physicians to make well-informed decisions regarding medication selection.

Physician-Pharmacist Collaboration-Ensuring Medication Compatibility:

In the prescription process, physicians and pharmacists work hand in hand. While doctors diagnose and prescribe, pharmacists, who are trained in medication therapy management and pharmacogenomics, play a pivotal role in assessing potential interactions between medications. This collaborative effort enhances patient safety by minimizing the risk of adverse reactions and optimizing the effectiveness of prescribed treatments.

Empowering Patients through Pharmacist Involvement:

Understanding the intricate dance of genetics and medications can be complex for patients. Having a licensed pharmacist involved in the process not only ensures accurate transmission of genetic information but also empowers patients with a knowledgeable ally. Some pharmacists can contribute to a more comprehensive and personalized approach to mental health care, fostering a sense of confidence and security in patients.

In summary, the collaboration between patients, healthcare providers, and licensed pharmacists is instrumental in unlocking the full potential of pharmacogenomics in mental health. People can navigate the complexities of personalized treatment with the help of pharmacists and doctors through seamless communication, ensuring a harmonious and successful dance between genetics and medications.

Does insurance cover pharmacogenomic testing?

Depending on your policy and reasons for testing, some insurance companies may or may not cover pharmacogenomic testing. **Contact your insurance provider about coverage prior to testing if this is a concern.**

Does Medicare cover pharmacogenomics?

Medicare coverage for PGx testing may vary depending on the region and the contractor that processes the claims. LCDs are Local Coverage Determinations, which are decisions made by a Medicare Administrative Contractor (MAC) on whether to cover a particular item or service in a MAC's jurisdiction.

For more information, please visit the <u>Mayo Clinic Center for Individualized Medicine.</u>

Session 1: Mental Health Q & A

After reading each section, you should be able to test your understanding by answering the following multiple-choice questions. Each question has four options, but only one is correct. You can check your answers with the answer key at the end of the exercise.

1. What is mental health?

    a) The absence of mental illness.
    b) The vital aspect of our well-being that affects how we think, feel, and act.
    c) The ability to perform daily tasks without any difficulty.
    d) The balance between positive and negative emotions.

2. What are common mental health issues for youth and adults?

    a) Anxiety, mood, psychotic, eating, substance, and personality disorders.
    b) Stress, anger, sadness, loneliness, boredom, and frustration.
    c) Learning disabilities, ADHD, autism, and dyslexia.
    d) Physical illnesses, injuries, pain, and disabilities.

3. What are anxiety disorders' signs and symptoms?

    a) Fear, nervousness, panic, phobias, OCD, social and general anxiety.
    b) Mood changes, depression, bipolar, dysthymia, and cyclothymia.
    c) Reality distortion, hallucinations, delusions, paranoia, and schizophrenia.
    d) Eating disorders, anorexia, bulimia, binge eating, and food avoidance.

Answers:

    1. b) The vital aspect of our well-being that affects how we think, feel, and act.
    2. a) Anxiety, mood, psychotic, eating, substance, and personality disorders.
    3. a) Fear, nervousness, panic, phobias, OCD, social and general anxiety.

Notes:
_____
_____

NOTES

MENTAL WELLNESS
Weekly log Guide

THINGS TO DO	Mon	Tue	Wed	Thu	Fri	Sat	Sun
MEDITATE	☐	☐	☐	☐	☐	☐	☐
EXERCISE	☐	☐	☐	☐	☐	☐	☐
EAT HEALTHY	☐	☐	☐	☐	☐	☐	☐
READ A BOOK	☐	☐	☐	☐	☐	☐	☐
TREAT YOURSELF	☐	☐	☐	☐	☐	☐	☐
SKINCARE ROUTINE	☐	☐	☐	☐	☐	☐	☐
SPEND FAMILY TIME	☐	☐	☐	☐	☐	☐	☐
TAKE A WALK OUTISDE	☐	☐	☐	☐	☐	☐	☐
WRITE IN MY JOURNAL	☐	☐	☐	☐	☐	☐	☐
HAVE FUN WITH HOBBIES	☐	☐	☐	☐	☐	☐	☐

WEEKLY REFLECTION NOTES:

SESSION 2
BUILDING A STRONG FOUNDATION

"You can purchase "SYM" T-shirts from our online store."

In this session, we will explore the importance of building a strong foundation for your mental health. We will discuss how your physical health affects your mental well-being, and how you can improve both by adopting a holistic approach. We will also help you develop self-awareness skills that will enable you to recognize and regulate your emotions and thoughts. Furthermore, we will introduce you to some effective coping mechanisms and stress management techniques that will help you deal with challenges and difficulties in life.

Finally, we will emphasize the value of positive relationships and support networks, and how you can cultivate them to enhance your mental health.

"A good mental foundation matter"

Notes:

_____
_____
_____
_____
_____
_____
_____
_____
_____

Building a strong foundation for your mental health can help you cope with challenges, achieve your goals, and enjoy life. Here are some ways to improve your mental health and why they are important:

a) The role of self-awareness is the ability to recognize and understand our feelings, thoughts, and behaviors. It can help us identify our strengths, weaknesses, values, and motivations. It can also help us manage our emotions, communicate effectively, and empathize with others. To improve our self-awareness, we can practice mindfulness, journaling, meditation, or therapy.

b) The mind-body connection and the impact of physical health on mental well-being. Our physical and mental health are closely linked, and each can influence the other.

For example, exercise can boost our mood, energy, and self-esteem, while chronic pain or illness can increase our stress, anxiety, and depression. Therefore, taking care of our physical health can benefit our mental health as well. This includes eating a balanced diet, getting enough sleep, staying hydrated, avoiding substance abuse, and seeking medical help when needed.

c) Developing healthy coping mechanisms and **stress management** techniques. Coping mechanisms are the strategies we use to deal with difficult situations or emotions. Stress management techniques are the ways we reduce or prevent stress from affecting us negatively. Healthy coping mechanisms and stress management techniques can help us cope with challenges, overcome obstacles, and bounce back from setbacks.

Some examples are breathing exercises, relaxation techniques, positive affirmations, problem-solving skills, time management skills, and hobbies.

d) Nurturing positive relationships and support networks involves the people we interact with regularly and who provide us with emotional, practical, or informational support. Positive relationships and support networks can help us feel loved, valued, and understood. They can also offer us guidance, feedback, encouragement, or assistance when we need it.

To nurture positive relationships and support networks, we can express gratitude, appreciation, and affection; listen actively and respectfully; give and receive constructive criticism; respect boundaries and preferences; ask for help when needed; and offer help when possible.

"The quality of our lives reflects the quality of our relationships and support networks. It is the source of joy, comfort, and growth. It's the mirror that reflects our true selves and the bridge that connects us to others and ourselves."

BUILD YOUR SUPPORT TEAM

Name :	Name :
Email :	Email :
Phone:	Phone:

Name :	Name :
Email :	Email :
Phone:	Phone:

Name :	Name :
Email :	Email :
Phone:	Phone:

Name :	Name :
Email :	Email :
Phone:	Phone:

Session 2: Building a Strong Foundation Q & A

Questions:

1. **What are the key components of a strong mental health foundation?**

    a) Regular exercise and junk food.
    b) A supportive social network, a balanced diet, and adequate sleep.
    c) Isolation and excessive screen time.
    d) Caffeine and late-night studying.

2. **Why is self-care important for maintaining good mental health?**

    a) It's not important at all.
    b) Self-care only benefits physical health.
    c) Self-care helps manage stress and promotes well-being.
    d) Self-care leads to overindulgence.

3. **What role does mindfulness play in building a strong foundation?**

    a) It doesn't play any role.
    b) Mindfulness increases stress.
    c) Mindfulness helps individuals reduce stress and enhance regulation.
    d) Offer help when possible.

Answers:

1. b) A supportive social network, a balanced diet, and adequate sleep.
2. c) Self-care helps manage stress and promotes well-being.
3. c) Mindfulness helps individuals reduce stress and enhance regulation.

Notes:

_____
_____
_____
_____
_____

NOTES

SESSION 3
CULTIVATING POSITIVE THINKING PATTERNS

CULTIVATING POSITIVE THINKING PATTERNS

"Peaches are good for your health, and so is positive thinking! It can improve your mood and your skills in any situation, while negative thinking can do the opposite."

In this section, we will explore how to cultivate positive thinking patterns that can boost your confidence, happiness, and resilience. We will learn how to:

1. Challenge negative self-talk and replace it with self-compassion. Negative self-talk is the inner critic that tells you that you are not good enough, smart enough, or worthy enough. Self-compassion is the ability to treat yourself with kindness, understanding, and forgiveness, especially when you face difficulties or failures.

2. Harness the power of positive affirmations and visualization. Positive affirmations are statements that affirm your strengths, abilities, and values. Visualization is the mental imagery of a desired outcome or situation. Both positive affirmations and visualization can help you shape your reality, overcome obstacles, and achieve your goals.

3. Practice gratitude and mindfulness to enhance your overall well-being. Gratitude is the appreciation of what you have and what others do for you. Mindfulness is the awareness of the present moment, without judgment or distraction. Both gratitude and mindfulness can help you reduce stress, increase joy, and improve your relationships.

4. Understand the importance of setting realistic goals and celebrating achievements. Set and celebrate realistic goals. Realistic goals are specific, measurable, attainable, relevant, and time-bound. Celebrating goals means rewarding your progress and effort. Both setting realistic goals and celebrating achievements can help you stay motivated, focused, and optimistic.

Session 3: Cultivating Positive Thinking Patterns Q & A

Questions:

1. How can one challenge and change negative thought patterns?

   a) Negative thoughts cannot be changed.
   b) By ignoring them.
   c) By identifying, evaluating, and replacing them with more positive alternatives.
   d) By suppressing them.

2. What are the benefits of practicing gratitude for mental health?

   a) It doesn't have any benefits.
   b) It can lead to increased stress.
   c) Gratitude can improve mood, life, and mental health.
   d) Gratitude is only relevant during holidays.

3. How does positive self-talk contribute to a healthier mindset?

   a) Positive self-talk has no impact on the mindset.
   b) It promotes self-criticism.
   c) Positive self-talk boosts self-esteem, resilience, and optimism.
   d) It leads to overconfidence.

Answers:

   1. c) By identifying, evaluating, and replacing them with more positive alternatives.
   2. c) Gratitude can improve mood, life, and mental health.
   3. c) Positive self-talk boosts self-esteem, resilience, and optimism.

Notes:
_____
_____
_____
_____

NOTES

SESSION 4
MANAGING ANXIETY AND STRESS

MANAGING ANXIETY AND STRESS

- Understanding anxiety and its triggers
- Techniques for managing and reducing anxiety
- Stress management strategies, including relaxation exercises and time management skills
- Creating a balanced lifestyle to minimize stress

Anxiety is a normal and adaptive response to perceived threats or challenges. However, when anxiety becomes excessive, persistent, or irrational, it can interfere with daily functioning and well-being. Some common triggers of anxiety are stressful life events, unrealistic expectations, negative self-talk, or physical health problems.

Many techniques can help manage and reduce anxiety, such as cognitive-behavioral therapy (CBT), exposure therapy, mindfulness meditation, breathing exercises, progressive muscle relaxation, or positive affirmations. These techniques can help challenge and change unhelpful thoughts, face, and overcome fears, calm the body and mind, and enhance self-esteem and coping skills.

"Anxiety is our natural reaction to what scares or challenges us. But when anxiety takes over our minds, it can ruin our lives. Anxiety can be triggered by many things, such as stress, expectations, self-criticism, or illness."

Stress is another common source of distress that can affect mental and physical health. Stress can be caused by external factors, such as work, family, or financial issues, or internal factors, such as personality traits, beliefs, or attitudes. Stress management strategies can help cope with stress in healthy and effective ways.

Managing anxiety and stress is not only beneficial for mental health, but also for physical health, emotional well-being, and overall quality of life. By learning and applying the techniques and strategies discussed in this chapter, one can gain more control over their anxiety and stress levels and improve their resilience and coping abilities.

"Breathe, relax, reflect, act."

Sessions 4: Managing Anxiety and Stress Q & A

Questions:

1. **What are some practical strategies for managing daily stress?**

    a) Avoiding social interactions.
    b) Deep breathing exercises and time management.
    c) Increasing caffeine intake.
    d) Ignoring stress completely.

2. **How does regular exercise help in reducing anxiety?**

    a) Exercise increases anxiety.
    b) Exercise releases endorphins, which reduce anxiety.
    c) Exercise has no impact on anxiety.
    d) Exercise only helps with physical health.

3. **What is mindfulness-based stress reduction, and how can it help anxiety?**

    a) It's a type of medication.
    b) Mindfulness-based stress reduction has no impact on anxiety.
    c) It uses meditation and lowers anxiety and stress.
    d) It's a form of intense physical exercise.

Answers:

1. b) Deep breathing exercises and time management.
2. b) Exercise releases endorphins, which reduce anxiety.
3. c) It uses meditation and lowers anxiety and stress.

Notes:

_____
_____
_____
_____
_____

NOTES

SESSION 5
ENHANCING EMOTIONAL INTELLIGENCE

ENHANCING EMOTIONAL INTELLIGENCE

Emotional Intelligence is the ability to recognize, understand, and manage one's own emotions, as well as the emotions of others. It is a crucial skill for personal and professional success, as it helps to build positive relationships, cope with stress, and handle conflicts.

In this section, we will explore the following aspects of emotional intelligence:

1. Identifying and understanding emotions: This involves being aware of the different types of emotions, such as happiness, sadness, anger, fear, and surprise, and how they affect our thoughts, behaviors, and decisions. We will also learn how to use tools such as the emotion wheel and the mood meter to label and measure our emotions more accurately.

2. Developing emotional regulation skills: This involves learning how to control and adjust our emotional responses to different situations, rather than being overwhelmed or reactive. We will also learn how to use strategies such as breathing exercises, mindfulness, positive self-talk, and reframing to calm ourselves down and cope with negative emotions.

3. Effective communication techniques for expressing emotions: This involves learning how to communicate our emotions clearly and respectfully, without hurting or offending others. We will learn active listening, assertiveness, and feedback to improve our communication with others.

4. Building empathy and understanding towards others: Empathy and understanding: This means seeing things from others' views and using skills like perspective-taking, validation, and compassion.

> **Key Signs of Emotional Intelligence:**
>
> Identifying and describing others' emotions | Self-confidence and self-acceptance | Letting go of mistakes | Empathy and concern for others | Accepting responsibility for errors | Managing emotions during challenging situations | Curiosity about people

Session 5: Enhancing Emotional Intelligence Q & A

Questions:

1. What is emotional intelligence, and why is it important for mental health?

    a) Emotional intelligence is irrelevant to mental health.
    b) It's the ability to recognize shapes and colors.
    c) Emotional intelligence helps us comprehend and control emotions.
    d) It's the ability to memorize facts and figures.

2. How can improving emotional awareness benefit personal relationships?

    a) It has no impact on personal relationships.
    b) Emotional awareness only causes conflicts.
    c) Emotional awareness helps connect and relate better.
    d) It makes people more distant.

3. What are some exercises to enhance emotional intelligence?

    a) Sudoku puzzles
    b) Listen, journal, and communicate empathetically.
    c) Physical fitness routines.
    d) Solving complex math problems.

Answer:

1. c) Emotional intelligence helps us comprehend and control emotions.
2. c) Emotional awareness helps connect and relate better.
3. b) Journal, listen, and communicate empathetically.

Notes:
_____
_____
_____
_____
_____

NOTES

SESSION 6
BUILDING RESILIENCE AND OVERCOMING CHALLENGES

BUILDING RESILIENCE AND OVERCOMING CHALLENGES

Resilience is the ability to cope with stress and adversity and to recover from negative experiences. Resilience is important for mental health because it helps people to maintain a positive outlook, adapt to changing circumstances, and overcome challenges. Resilience is not a fixed trait that some people have, and others don't.

> *"Resilience does not mean avoiding challenges but embracing them."*

It can be **learned** and **developed** through various strategies, such as:

1. Building supportive relationships with family, friends, and community members who can provide emotional and practical support.

2. Practicing self-care by taking care of your physical, emotional, and ethical needs, including getting enough sleep, eating well, exercising, meditating, etc.

3. Develop a growth mindset by viewing difficulties as opportunities to learn and grow, rather than failures or threats.

4. Seeking professional help when needed and recognizing the importance of therapy. Therapy can help you identify and address your stress's underlying causes, develop coping skills, and enhance your well-being.

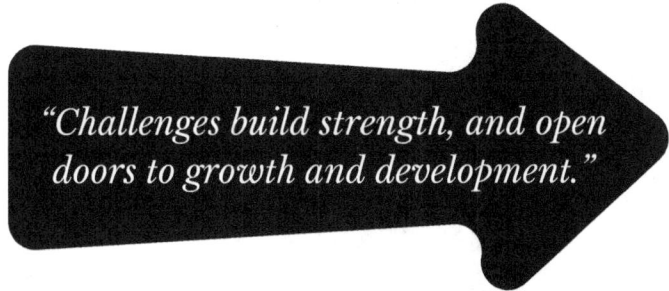

"Challenges build strength, and open doors to growth and development."

The examples of resilience in action and how people can adapt to challenging situations and overcome them are:

- A student who fails an exam but studies harder for the next one and seeks feedback from the teacher on how to improve is resilient because they do not give up on their academic goals. **They use the failure as a learning opportunity and take positive actions to improve their performance.**

- A worker who loses their job, but uses their network to find new opportunities and learn new skills to increase their employability, is resilient because they do not let the job loss affect their self-esteem or motivation. **They use their social resources and personal initiative to find new ways to earn a living.**

- A person who experiences a traumatic event but seeks counseling and joins a support group to process their emotions and heal is resilient because they do not let the trauma define them or isolate them. **They seek professional and social support to deal with their feelings and move forward with their lives.**

- A parent who faces a divorce but focuses on the best interests of their children and co-parents effectively with their ex-partner is resilient because they do not let the divorce affect their parenting or their relationship with their children. **They prioritize the well-being of their family and cooperate with their ex-partner to provide a stable and supportive environment for their children.**

> *"The way we respond to challenges when they arise matters more than the challenges themselves."*

Session 6: Building Resilience and Overcoming Challenges Q & A

Questions:

1. What is resilience, and why is it important in mental health?

    a) Resilience is unimportant in mental health.
    b) Resilience is the ability to avoid all challenges.
    c) Resilience is bouncing back and adapting to challenges.
    d) Resilience is the same as stubbornness.

2. How can one develop resilience in the face of adversity?

    a) By avoiding adversity at all costs.
    b) By pretending adversity doesn't exist.
    c) Resilience means having good relationships, optimism, and coping skills.
    d) Resilience is innate and cannot be developed.

3. What role does self-compassion play in building resilience?

    a) Self-compassion has no role in building resilience.
    b) Self-compassion is a sign of weakness.
    c) Self-compassion is being kind and understanding to oneself.
    d) Self-compassion is only relevant in relationships.

Answers:

    1. c) Resilience is bouncing back and adapting to challenges.
    2. c) Resilience means having good relationships, optimism, and coping skills.
    3. c) Self-compassion is being kind and understanding to oneself.

Notes:

_____
_____
_____
_____

NOTES

SESSION 7
NAVIGATING SOCIAL MEDIA AND DIGITAL WELL-BEING

NAVIGATING SOCIAL MEDIA AND DIGITAL WELL-BEING

Social media can have both positive and negative effects on our mental health. On one hand, it can help us connect with others, share our interests, and express ourselves. On the other hand, it can also expose us to unrealistic expectations, negative feedback, and online harassment. Therefore, it is important to be aware of how social media affects us and to take steps to protect our well-being.

One way to do this is to **establish healthy boundaries** and **manage our screen time**:

- Limit social media use and choose wisely.
- Take social media breaks and do other activities.
- Enrich lives with hobbies, exercise, friends, and family.

Ways to promote digital well-being is to practice mindfulness and self-care.

Mindfulness is the ability to pay attention to the present moment without judgment.

> It can help us cope with stress, anxiety, and negative emotions that may arise from social media use.

Self-care is the act of taking care of our physical, emotional, and mental health.

> It can include activities such as meditation, yoga, reading, or listening to music.

Finally, you can foster healthy online relationships and combat cyberbullying by being respectful, supportive, and empathetic towards others. You can also report or block abusive or harmful content or users that you encounter on social media. You can also seek help from trusted adults or professionals if you experience or witness cyberbullying or any other form of online violence.

Session 7: Navigating Social Media and Digital Well-being Q & A

Questions:

1. How does excessive use of social media impact mental health?

a) Excessive use of social media has no impact on mental health.
b) It improves mental health.
c) It causes loneliness, anxiety, low self-esteem, and poor mental health.
d) Excessive social media use is a sign of good mental health.

2. How to balance social media and well-being?

a) There are no strategies for balancing social media and well-being.
b) Limit time, create positivity, and detox digitally.
c) Spending all waking hours on social media.
d) Avoiding social media altogether.

3. How can we foster healthy online relationships?

a) Individuals cannot protect their mental health online.
b) By engaging in cyberbullying.
c) Be aware, report cyberbullying, and block abusive content or users.
d) To ignore online interactions.

Answers:

1. c) It causes loneliness, anxiety, low self-esteem, and poor mental health.
2. b) Limit time, create positivity, and detox digitally.
3. c) Be aware, report cyberbullying, and block abusive content or users.

Notes:
_____
_____
_____
_____

NOTES

SESSION 8
YOUTH MENTAL HEALTH

YOUTH MENTAL HEALTH

Youth mental health is a critical topic as it encompasses the mental well-being of individuals during their adolescent and teenage years. This period is characterized by significant physical, emotional, and cognitive changes, making it a time of both growth and vulnerability. Here are some key aspects to consider when exploring youth and mental health in more detail:

1. Prevalence and Impact: Many young people struggle with mental health issues, especially depression and anxiety. If not treated, these issues can harm their school, social, and personal lives.

2. Unique Challenges: Adolescence is a transitional period marked by various challenges. Youth face increasing pressures related to. These challenges, combined with hormonal changes and brain development, can affect their mental health:

- Academic performance - peer relationships
- Identity formation - body image - societal expectations

3. Risk Factors: Mental health problems in youth can be influenced by:

- Family history of mental illness and traumatic experiences
- Chronic medical conditions—substance abuse
- Bullying—stigma, social isolation, discrimination
- Low socioeconomic status—lack of mental health resources

4. Common Disorders: Youth often face mental disorders. The disorders include:

- Anxiety disorders (e.g., generalized anxiety disorder and social anxiety disorder, eating disorders, and bipolar disorder)
- Self-harm behaviors, substance abuse, depression, and ADHD

5. Warning Signs: Recognize the warning signs of mental health issues in youth.

- Persistent sadness or irritability
- Significant changes in sleep or appetite
- Withdrawal from activities or social interactions
- Difficulty concentrating
- Sudden decline in academic performance
- Increased risk-taking behaviors
- Self-harm or talk of suicide

6. Support and Interventions: Stigma-free environment for youth. **Before intervening, consult a MEDICAL PROFESSIONAL.**

- Provide access to mental health resources that suit their needs.
- Possible interventions are:
    - Therapy (individual, family, or CBT)
    - Medication when needed
    - Support groups
    - School-based mental health programs

Notes:

_____
_____
_____
_____
_____
_____

The CDC says 20% of children have a mental disorder yearly. Childhood mental disorders cost $247 billion annually. Common ones are ADHD, Anxiety, Behavior, and Depression.

Mental disorders differ by age and country. US children aged 3-17 years had these diagnoses in 2016-2019:

- ADHD: 9.8% (6.0 million)
- Anxiety: 9.4% (5.8 million)
- Behavior: 8.9% (5.5 million)
- Depression: 4.4% (2.7 million)

Many children have multiple mental disorders. For example, 75% of depressed children also have anxiety, and 50% have behavior problems. Child mental health is a global crisis that affects millions of children. Here are some sources to learn more:

- CDC: Data and Statistics on Children's Mental Health
- Children's mental health is in crisis
- AAFP: Study: One in Six U.S. Children Has a Mental Illness
- CDC: Child Mental Health
- Research Update: Children's Anxiety and Depression on the Rise

It is crucial to prioritize the mental health of young people and provide them with the necessary support and resources to navigate the challenges they face. Early identification, intervention, and destigmatization play key roles in promoting positive mental well-being and ensuring a healthy transition into adulthood.

Notes:

_____
_____
_____
_____
_____
_____

CHILDREN WITH MENTAL HEALTH CHALLENGES IN DISADVANTAGED COMMUNITIES

Mental health can have a significant impact on children in disadvantaged communities. Disadvantaged communities often face various socioeconomic challenges, including poverty, limited access to quality education, inadequate healthcare, higher crime rates, and social inequality. These factors can contribute to increased stress, trauma, and adverse childhood experiences, which can have profound effects on a child's mental well-being.

Here are some specific ways in which mental health can affect kids in disadvantaged communities:

1. Higher prevalence of mental health disorders:

- Children in disadvantaged communities are more likely to have mental health disorders.
- Disorders include anxiety, depression, PTSD, and conduct disorders.
- Causes include chronic stressors, violence, unstable living conditions, and limited mental health services.

2. Limited access to mental health resources:

- Disadvantaged communities face barriers to resources.
- Shortage of mental health professionals in these communities.
- Financial constraints and lack of health insurance coverage.
- Families may not seek or lack proper mental health care for children.

"Children in disadvantaged communities experience higher rates of mental health disorders."

3. Increased trauma exposure:

- Children in disadvantaged communities face more traumatic events, such as violence, abuse, neglect, and community violence.
- Symptoms: Hypervigilance, nightmares, flashbacks, and concentration problems.
- Impact: This can damage a child's mental and emotional well-being.

4. Academic challenges:

- Mental health issues can impair a child's academic performance.
- They can affect concentration, memory, and motivation, resulting in lower achievement.
- This can worsen the cycle of disadvantage, as education is key to escaping poverty.

5. Social and emotional difficulties:

- Mental health problems can affect a child's social interactions and emotional well-being.
- Children may have trouble with relationships, behavior, and low self-esteem.
- These challenges can isolate them from support and worsen their mental health issues.

6. Long-term consequences:

- Childhood mental health issues can have lasting effects if untreated.
- Children may struggle with mental health problems throughout their lives.
- This can affect their education, work, and quality of life.

A comprehensive approach is needed to address mental health challenges in disadvantaged communities. Strategies should improve access to mental health services, implement trauma-informed care in schools and communities, promote early intervention and prevention programs, and address social determinants of mental health (e.g., poverty and inequality).

Supporting the mental health of children in disadvantaged communities can reduce the negative impact and improve their well-being and success.

HOW MENTAL HEALTH CHALLENGES AFFECT CHILDREN IN SCHOOL

Mental health significantly affects children in school, influencing their academic performance, social interactions, and overall well-being. Here are several ways in which mental health can impact children in the school setting:

1. Academic performance:
Mental health issues can have a detrimental effect on a child's academic performance. Conditions like anxiety, depression, ADHD, and learning disabilities can impair concentration, memory, and cognition. Reduced motivation, low self-esteem, and feelings of hopelessness can also contribute to decreased academic achievement.

2. Concentration and focus: Mental health problems can make it challenging for children to concentrate and maintain focus in the classroom. Attention difficulties, restlessness, and intrusive thoughts can disrupt their ability to engage with lessons, complete assignments, and participate actively in class discussions. As a result, their learning and comprehension may be compromised.

3. Attendance and participation: Mental health issues can lead to absenteeism and reduced participation in school activities. Children may experience difficulties getting out of bed, going to school, or engaging in social interactions due to symptoms of anxiety, depression, or other mental health conditions. This can result in missed classes, falling behind on coursework, and isolation from their peers.

> **It's crucial that we prioritize mental health support for our young ones to create a healthier environment in schools.**

4. Social interactions and relationships: Mental health problems can impact a child's social interactions and relationships with peers and teachers. Social anxiety, low self-esteem, or behavioral difficulties associated with mental health conditions can make it challenging for children to initiate and maintain friendships, collaborate with classmates, and seek help from teachers. This can contribute to feelings of isolation, loneliness, and a lack of social support, further exacerbating their mental health struggles.

5. Bullying and victimization: Children with mental health issues may be more vulnerable to bullying and victimization by their peers. Their struggles may make them targets for bullying, leading to additional emotional distress and worsening of their mental health symptoms. This hostile environment can further negatively impact their school experience and well-being.

6. Educational transitions: Transitions within the educational system, such as starting a new school, changing grade levels, or transitioning to higher education, can be particularly challenging for children with mental health issues. These transitions often involve new environments, increased academic demands, and changes in social dynamics, which can exacerbate anxiety, stress, and adjustment difficulties.

It is important to promote awareness and destigmatization of mental health...

A comprehensive approach with educators, school administrators, mental health professionals, and parents is needed to address mental health in schools. They should promote awareness and destigmatization of mental health, provide resources and support services in schools, train teachers to recognize and respond to mental health concerns, and foster a positive and inclusive school climate for student well-being. This can support children's academic success, social development, and mental well-being.

HOW SCHOOLS CAN HELP CHILDREN WITH MENTAL HEALTH CHALLENGES

Schools can play a crucial role in supporting the mental health of children. Here are some ways in which schools can help:

1. Promoting mental health awareness: Schools can educate students, teachers, and staff about mental health, its importance, and common mental health conditions. This can help reduce stigma, increase understanding, and create an environment that supports mental well-being.

2. Providing access to mental health resources: Schools can offer access to mental health resources within the school setting. This may include on-site counseling services, school psychologists, or partnerships with community mental health organizations. Schools can also provide information about external mental health services and facilitate referrals when necessary.

3. Training for educators: Teachers and staff can receive training on recognizing signs of mental health issues in students. This training can help them identify when a student might be struggling and provide appropriate support or referrals. Educators can also learn strategies to create a supportive and inclusive classroom environment that promotes positive mental health.

4. Implementing mental health curriculum: Schools can incorporate mental health education into the curriculum, teaching students about topics such as emotional regulation, stress management, and building resilience. This can help students develop coping skills and promote their overall mental well-being.

5. Creating a positive and inclusive school climate: Schools can foster a positive and inclusive environment that promotes mental health. This includes promoting kindness, empathy, and respect among students, addressing bullying and discrimination, and encouraging peer support networks. School-wide events, campaigns, and clubs focused on mental health can also help raise awareness and create a sense of community.

6. Supporting transitions and managing stress: Schools can provide support during educational transitions, such as starting a new school or transitioning to higher grades. They can also implement strategies to help students manage stress, such as providing study skills workshops, teaching stress reduction techniques, and offering outlets for physical activity and relaxation.

7. Collaborating with families: Schools can work closely with families to support students' mental health. This may involve regular communication, sharing information about available resources, and involving parents or guardians in the development of individualized support plans for students with mental health needs.

8. Creating a safe and supportive physical environment: Schools can ensure that the physical environment is safe, welcoming, and conducive to positive mental health. This includes addressing issues such as bullying, violence, and substance abuse, as well as promoting healthy habits like regular exercise, nutritious meals, and adequate sleep.

9. Providing peer support programs: Schools can establish peer support programs where students can seek support from trained peers. These programs can create a sense of belonging, reduce feelings of isolation, and provide a safe space for students to discuss their mental health concerns.

10. Collaborating with community partners: Schools can collaborate with community organizations, mental health professionals, and local agencies to expand the range of mental health services available to students. This can involve partnerships for counseling services, workshops, and prevention programs.

By implementing these strategies, schools can contribute to creating a supportive and nurturing environment that promotes the mental health and well-being of their students.

CHILDREN WHO DO NOT RECEIVE APPROPRIATE HELP FOR THEIR MENTAL HEALTH NEEDS AT A YOUNG AGE

Without early help for mental health, children may face these risks:

1. Academic Challenges: Mental health issues affect children's focus, learning, and grades. They need support or they may struggle in school and do worse academically.

2. Social and Relationship Difficulties: Mental health issues can cause trouble with friends, relationships, or social cues. This can cause isolation, loneliness, and low self-esteem.

3. Emotional Distress: Mental health problems can make children feel sad, anxious, angry, or irritable for a long time. This can hurt their well-being and quality of life.

4. Behavioral Problems: Children with unaddressed mental health issues may exhibit challenging behaviors such as aggression, impulsivity, or withdrawal. These behaviors can disrupt their daily functioning, strain relationships, and potentially lead to disciplinary actions or conflicts.

5. Physical Health Issues: Mental health problems can also have physical health implications. Children may experience changes in appetite, sleep disturbances, headaches, or other physical symptoms related to stress and emotional distress.

> *Mental health issues in childhood can persist into adolescence and adulthood, potentially exacerbating their impact....*

6. Long-Term Impact: If left untreated, mental health issues in childhood can persist into adolescence and adulthood, potentially exacerbating their impact. Untreated mental health problems in childhood can increase the risk of developing more severe mental health disorders later in life.

7. Risky Behaviors: Children who don't receive appropriate support for their mental health needs may be at a higher risk of engaging in risky behaviors, such as substance abuse, self-harm, or delinquency. These behaviors can have serious consequences for their overall well-being and prospects.

It's important to recognize the signs of mental health issues in children and seek professional help when needed. Early intervention and appropriate support can make a significant difference in a child's well-being, development, and long-term outcomes.

HEALTHY EATING TIPS FOR CHILDREN WITH MENTAL HEALTH CHALLENGES

Encouraging healthy eating and exercise habits in children is important for their overall well-being. Here are some tips for promoting healthy eating and exercise:

1. Be a Role Model: Children often learn by observing their parents and caregivers. Be a positive role model by practicing healthy eating habits and engaging in regular physical activity yourself.

2. Make Healthy Foods Fun: Present fruits, vegetables, whole grains, and lean proteins in creative and appealing ways. Use colorful plates, arrange food in fun shapes, and involve children in meal preparation to make healthy eating enjoyable.

3. Offer a Variety of Foods: Introduce a wide range of nutritious foods to children. Encourage them to try new fruits, vegetables, and whole grains. Offer different options to provide a balanced and diverse diet.

Please consult with a medical professional before trying the exercises.

"Be a positive role model by practicing healthy eating yourself."

Notes:

_____
_____
_____
_____
_____
_____
_____
_____

4. Limit Processed Foods and Sugary Drinks: Minimize the consumption of processed foods, sugary snacks, and beverages. Instead, opt for fresh, whole foods and encourage water or milk as the primary drinks.

5. Establish Regular Mealtimes: Set consistent meal times that allow for family meals whenever possible. Eating together promotes healthy eating habits and creates a positive and supportive environment.

6. Encourage Physical Activity: Encourage children to exercise regularly. Make it enjoyable by participating in activities they enjoy, such as swimming, cycling, dancing, or playing games outdoors.

7. Limit Sedentary Activities: Limit screen time and sedentary activities, such as watching television or playing video games. Encourage children to engage in active play, sports, or hobbies that get them moving.

"*Cooking and eating together promotes healthy eating habits and creates a positive and supportive environment.*"

8. Make Exercise Fun: Find creative ways to make exercise enjoyable. Incorporate activities that children find exciting, such as going for family walks, playing active games, or having dance parties.

9. Set Realistic Goals: Help children set realistic goals for healthy eating and exercise. Focus on small, achievable steps rather than drastic changes. Celebrate their progress and provide positive reinforcement.

Remember, it's important to tailor these exercises to the child's age and developmental level. Additionally, if a child is experiencing significant mental health challenges, it's recommended to seek professional help from a mental health provider.

Notes:

_____
_____
_____
_____
_____

PROMOTING MENTAL HEALTH: EXERCISES AND TIPS FOR CHILDREN

Promoting mental health exercise tips for children is a great way to support their emotional well-being. Here are some exercises and activities that can help children develop and maintain good mental health:

1. Mindful Breathing: Teach children the practice of deep breathing to calm their minds and bodies. Encourage them to take slow, deep breaths, focusing on the sensation of air entering and leaving their bodies.

2. Gratitude Journaling: Encourage children to keep a gratitude journal, where they write down things they are grateful for each day. This exercise promotes positive thinking and helps them develop a sense of appreciation.

3. Exercise and Physical Activity: Engaging in regular physical activity is not only good for physical health but also has positive effects on mental well-being. Encourage children to participate in activities they enjoy, such as sports, dancing, or yoga.

4. Creative Expression: Encourage children to express themselves creatively through art, music, or writing. These activities can serve as outlets for their emotions and help them process and understand their feelings.

5. Mindfulness Activities: Teach children calming routines like sensory walks, breathing buddies, or quiet reflection to help them feel grounded and more in tune with their emotions. These activities can help children become more aware of their thoughts, emotions, and physical sensations. Over time, these routines can build emotional resilience and give children tools to manage stress. Practicing mindfulness regularly also supports focus, self-regulation, and a stronger sense of inner calm.

6. Social Connections: Encourage children to maintain positive social connections with friends and family members. Engaging in activities together, such as playing games, having conversations, or sharing hobbies, can promote a sense of belonging and emotional well-being.

7. Self-Care: Teach children the importance of self-care and help them develop self-care routines. This can include activities such as taking a warm bath, reading a book, spending time in nature, or engaging in hobbies they enjoy.

8. Positive Affirmations: Encourage children to practice positive self-talk and use affirmations to boost their self-esteem. Teach them to replace negative thoughts with positive ones and to recognize their strengths and accomplishments.

9. Mindful Eating: Teach children about mindful eating, which involves paying attention to the sensory experience of eating, such as the taste, texture, and smell of food. Please encourage them to eat slowly, savor each bite, and be aware of their hunger and fullness cues.

10. Relaxation Techniques: Teach children relaxation techniques such as progressive muscle relaxation or guided imagery. These techniques can help them relax their bodies and minds, reducing stress and anxiety.

Remember, it's important to tailor these exercises to the child's age and developmental level. Additionally, if a child is experiencing significant mental health challenges, it's recommended to seek professional help from a mental health provider.

Q & A GUIDE FOR PARENTS OR ANYONE CARING FOR CHILDREN WITH MENTAL HEALTH CHALLENGES

Q: How can I support my child with mental illness?

A: Supporting a child with mental illness requires a multifaceted approach. Here are some strategies you can consider:

1. Educate yourself: Learn about your child's specific mental illness, its symptoms, and available treatments. This will help you understand what your child is going through and how to provide appropriate support.

2. Encourage open communication: Create a safe environment where your child feels comfortable discussing their feelings and experiences. Active listening and non-judgmental attitudes can make a significant difference in their willingness to share.

3. Seek professional help: Consult with mental health professionals who specialize in your child's condition. They can provide an accurate diagnosis, recommend appropriate treatments, and offer guidance on managing the illness.

4. Establish routines and structure: Consistency and predictability can be beneficial for children with mental illness. Establish regular routines for meals, sleep, and daily activities to provide stability and reduce anxiety.

5. Encourage healthy habits: Promote a healthy lifestyle by encouraging physical activity, proper nutrition, and sufficient sleep. These factors contribute to overall well-being and can positively impact mental health.

6. Foster a supportive network: Connect with support groups, both online and offline, for parents of children with mental illness. Sharing experiences, challenges, and coping strategies with others who understand can be immensely helpful.

7. Be patient and flexible: Understand that recovery takes time, and setbacks may occur. Practice patience and flexibility while supporting your child through their journey.

Q: How can I help my child manage their emotions?

A: Helping your child manage their emotions is vital for their well-being.

Here are some strategies you can try:

1. Teach emotional awareness: Help your child identify and label their emotions. Encourage them to express their feelings healthily and constructively.

2. Foster open communication: Create a safe space for your child to discuss their emotions. Listen attentively, validate their feelings, and avoid judgment or criticism.

3. Teach coping skills: Explore and practice coping strategies together. These may include deep breathing exercises, journaling, engaging in hobbies, or seeking support from trusted individuals.

4. Encourage self-care: Teach your child the importance of self-care activities, such as getting enough sleep, eating well, and engaging in activities they enjoy. These practices can help regulate emotions.

5. Model healthy emotional regulation: Be a positive role model by healthily managing your emotions. Children often learn by observing their parents' behavior.

6. Provide a structured environment: Establish routines and clear expectations to create a sense of stability and security. Consistency can help children feel more in control of their emotions.

7. Seek professional help if needed: If your child's emotions significantly impact their daily functioning or cause distress, consider consulting a mental health professional for additional support and guidance.

Remember, supporting your child's emotional well-being is an ongoing process. It's important to adapt your approach based on their individual needs and, if needed, seek professional help when necessary.

MENTAL HEALTH HELP FOR CHILDREN

If you are a parent seeking mental health help for your child, there are several steps you can take:

1. Recognize the signs: Pay attention to any noticeable changes in your child's behavior, emotions, or functioning. Signs of potential mental health issues may include persistent sadness, anxiety, withdrawal from activities, changes in sleep or appetite, difficulty concentrating, or a decline in school performance.

2. Consult with a pediatrician: Start by scheduling an appointment with your child's pediatrician. They can assess your child's physical health and determine whether a mental health evaluation is necessary. Pediatricians often know of local mental health resources and can refer you to appropriate specialists.

3. Seek professional help: Depending on the severity of the situation, you may need to consult a mental health professional, such as a child psychologist, psychiatrist, or therapist. These professionals specialize in diagnosing and treating mental health concerns in children. You can ask for referrals from your pediatrician, school counselors, or trusted friends and family members.

4. Contact your insurance provider: If you have health insurance, review your policy to understand the coverage for mental health services. Contact your insurance provider or check their website to find a list of approved mental health professionals in your network. This can help you narrow down your options and minimize out-of-pocket expenses.

5. Research local resources: Look for community mental health centers, counseling centers, or child psychiatry clinics in your area. These organizations often provide mental health services specifically for children and adolescents. They may offer counseling, therapy, and psychiatric evaluations. Check their websites or call them directly to inquire about their services and appointment availability.

6. Involve your child's school: Reach out to your child's school counselor or psychologist for assistance. They can provide valuable insights into your child's behavior and academic performance and may offer resources or referrals to mental health professionals who work with children.

7. Support groups and online communities: Seek support groups or online communities for parents of children with mental health challenges. These groups can provide emotional support, share experiences, and offer advice on navigating the mental health system.

Remember, early intervention is crucial in addressing mental health issues in children. Trust your instincts as a parent, and don't hesitate to seek help when you feel your child may be struggling.

Choosing the right mental health professional for children.

Getting a mental health professional who can relate to a child's culture, background, race, religion, and other relevant aspects of their identity is incredibly important for several reasons:

1. Cultural sensitivity: Mental health professionals who understand and respect a child's cultural background can provide more culturally sensitive and appropriate care. They are better equipped to recognize how cultural factors may influence a child's experiences, values, beliefs, and attitudes toward mental health. This understanding can help ensure that the treatment approaches and interventions align with the child's cultural context, increasing the effectiveness of therapy.

2. Trust and rapport: When a child sees a professional who shares their cultural or ethnic background, they may feel more comfortable. Building trust and rapport with a therapist is crucial for effective therapy, and having a professional who can relate to the child's cultural experiences can facilitate this process. It can create a safe space where the child feels free to express themselves without fear of judgment or misunderstanding.

3. Language and communication: Language is important for therapy. Children may prefer their native language. A professional who speaks the same language can communicate and understand better, reducing the potential for miscommunication or misinterpretation.

4. Addressing unique challenges: Different cultural backgrounds and identities can bring unique challenges and stressors that may impact a child's mental health. For example, experiences of discrimination, acculturation stress, or intergenerational conflicts may be specific to certain cultural or ethnic groups. A professional who understands these challenges can provide targeted support and interventions to address them effectively.

5. Family involvement: In many cultures, family plays a significant role in a child's mental health and well-being. Mental health professionals who have cultural competence can better engage with the child's family and involve them in the therapeutic process. They can consider the family's beliefs, practices, and values, and work collaboratively with them to support the child's mental health.

Summary: It's important to note that:

- Finding a perfect cultural or ethnic match may not be possible.
- Seek a professional who is culturally competent, open, and willing to learn.
- Professionals should understand the child's unique experiences.
- The best options are pediatricians, child psychologists, psychiatrists, and therapists.

There can be several reasons why some mental health professionals choose not to work with children:

1. Specialization: Mental health professionals may specialize in different age groups or populations. They may have received specialized training, certifications, or experience that make them better equipped to work with certain age groups.

2. Personal preference: Working with children requires special skills and personality. Some mental health professionals prefer working with adults. They need to work within their areas of expertise and interest to provide the best possible care.

3. Training limitations: Some mental health professionals receive training in different areas. Child psychology and child development require specialized knowledge and techniques that may not be covered in the training of all mental health professionals.

4. Legal and ethical considerations: Working with children poses legal and ethical challenges for mental health professionals. They need parental consent, confidentiality, and compliance with rules for minors. Some professionals may choose to avoid these complexities by focusing solely on adult clients.

5. Personal resources: Children need different levels of support and resources than adults. This includes therapy spaces, tools, and interventions for kids. Some mental health professionals may not have the resources or infrastructure to help children well.

"It is important to find appropriate professionals who are qualified and willing to work with children."

NOTES

GLOBAL ORGANIZATIONS THAT FOCUS ON MENTAL HEALTH FOR CHILDREN

SOME ORGANIZATIONS THAT FOCUS ON MENTAL HEALTH FOR CHILDREN

National Alliance on Mental Illness (NAMI) is a national organization that focuses on mental health for children in the United States. While NAMI serves people of all ages, it also provides resources designed for children and adolescents. NAMI offers support, education, advocacy, and awareness programs to improve mental health and well-being.

Child Mind Institute is a nonprofit organization in the United States dedicated to transforming the lives of children struggling with mental health and learning disorders. They provide clinical care, conduct research, offer educational resources, and advocate for policy change to support children's mental health.

Canadian Mental Health Association (CMHA) Canada, promotes mental health and helps people of all ages, including children and youth. CMHA has programs and services across the country for children with mental health issues.

Many countries have their own organizations for children's mental health. You should research and find local resources and organizations for more support.

Please be persistent when contacting these agencies. Don't stop at the first door. Keep knocking until a door opens.

There are several **GLOBAL** mental health hotlines and helplines that provide support and assistance to individuals in need. Here are a few examples from different countries:

1. United States: The National Suicide Prevention Lifeline is a 24/7 hotline that provides free and confidential support to individuals in distress, including those experiencing mental health crises. You can reach them at 1-800-273-TALK (1-800-273-8255). **https://www.samhsa.gov/find-help/988**

2. United Kingdom: The Samaritans is a helpline available 24/7 for individuals in the UK and Ireland who are in need of emotional support. You can contact them at 116 123. **https://www.samaritans.org/how-we-can-help/if-youre-having-difficult-time/**

3. Canada: Crisis Services Canada operates a national suicide prevention and mental health support hotline available 24/7. You can reach them at 1-833-456-4566. **https://crtc.gc.ca/eng/phone/988.htm**

4. Australia: Lifeline Australia provides 24/7 crisis support and suicide prevention services. You can contact them at 13 11 14. **https://www.lifeline.org.au/**

5. India: Vandrevala Foundation Helpline is a mental health helpline in India that offers support and counseling services. Their helpline number is +91-1860-2662-345. **https://www.vandrevalafoundation.com/**

Please note that these are just a few examples, and there may be other hotlines and helplines available in your country or region. It's always a good idea to search for local mental health hotlines or consult the resources provided by national mental health agencies for the most up-to-date and relevant information.

Remember to check out our mental wellness resources on our website www.peachesandcream.org. We offer podcasts, YouTube videos, and more information to help you cope with stress, anxiety, and other challenges.

HOW MENTORSHIP CAN HELP CHILDREN WITH MENTAL HEALTH CHALLENGES

Mentorship can be especially beneficial for children with mental health problems. Here's how mentorship can help:

1. Emotional support: Mentors provide a safe and non-judgmental space for children to express their feelings and concerns related to their mental health. Having a mentor who empathizes with their struggles can offer much-needed emotional support.

2. Coping strategies: Mentors can share practical coping strategies and techniques to help children manage their mental health challenges.

3. Self-esteem and self-acceptance: Mentors can help children develop a positive self-image and self-acceptance. By focusing on their strengths and encouraging self-care practices, mentors can improve a child's self-esteem and resilience.

"Mentors can help empower children and assist them with mental health needs."

4. Goal-setting and motivation: Mentors can assist children in setting realistic goals related to their mental health management. They can provide guidance and support in creating action plans, monitoring progress, and celebrating achievements, fostering motivation and a sense of accomplishment. By modeling consistency and empathy, mentors help children build confidence and develop lifelong self-care habits.

5. Advocacy and empowerment: Mentors can empower children to advocate for their mental health needs. They can help children understand their rights, navigate support systems, and communicate effectively with healthcare professionals, teachers, and other relevant individuals.

6. Social connection and community engagement: Mentors can help children build social connections and engage in activities that promote their mental well-being. They can introduce children to support groups, community resources, and positive peer networks, reducing feelings of isolation and fostering a sense of belonging.

7. Education and awareness: Mentors can educate children about mental health conditions, reducing stigma and promoting a better understanding of their own experiences. This knowledge can empower children to seek help, engage in self-care, and make informed decisions about their mental health.

Visit our website www.peachesandcream.org to learn more about our mentorship program and how to enroll your child. Our main focus is on girls aged 11-17, but we also offer some services for boys.

CONCLUSION

Thank you for reading this book on Mental Health for Youth and Adults. We hope you found it useful and informative. We are here to support you and anyone who has this book in their possession. That is why we created this book and other books and resources to help you cope with mental health challenges. We appreciate your help in spreading our message and reaching out to the children and others who need our assistance. That is why our services and resources are affordable and at little to no cost. Because we are here to help, not for financial gain.

Ways you can get involved with the Peaches and Cream Foundation Mental Wellness Movement:

- Volunteering your time and expertise in events, workshops, and programs
- Donating to our organization online or offline
- Spreading awareness on social media, blog, or community
- Hosting an event or fundraiser with your own theme or activity
- Purchasing merchandise from our online store

For more information or to join our movement, please visit our website at www.peachesandcream.org and click on the mental wellness page. We would love to hear from you and have you on board.

MENTAL WELLNESS CHALLENGE AND PLANNERS

"**On the next pages,** you will find a 5-day mental wellness challenge and a daily, weekly, and 90-day planner to help you start with small goals and achieve bigger ones."

Be sure to grab the Support Your Mental (SYM) workbook and planner on Amazon, and explore additional SYM resources and templates by visiting our online store at www.peachesandcream.org—just click the "Shop" tab to browse.

Writing is a powerful tool for healing, growth, and happiness, and it is a beneficial activity for mental health, as it can help you:

- Express your emotions
- Process your thoughts
- Increase your self-awareness
- Reduce stress, anxiety, and depression
- Improve your mood, confidence, and well-being

Writing in a planner can also help you:

- Improve your memory
- Increase your accountability
- Organize your goals and tasks
- Schedule your time and deadlines
- Review and adjust your plans

Writing down your challenges can also help you:

- Identify and understand your problems
- Find solutions and strategies
- Overcome obstacles and setbacks
- Learn from your mistakes and failures
- Celebrate your achievements and successes

"Writing down challenges and using a planner transforms overwhelm into clarity—each page becomes proof that progress is possible."

5-DAY CHALLENGE

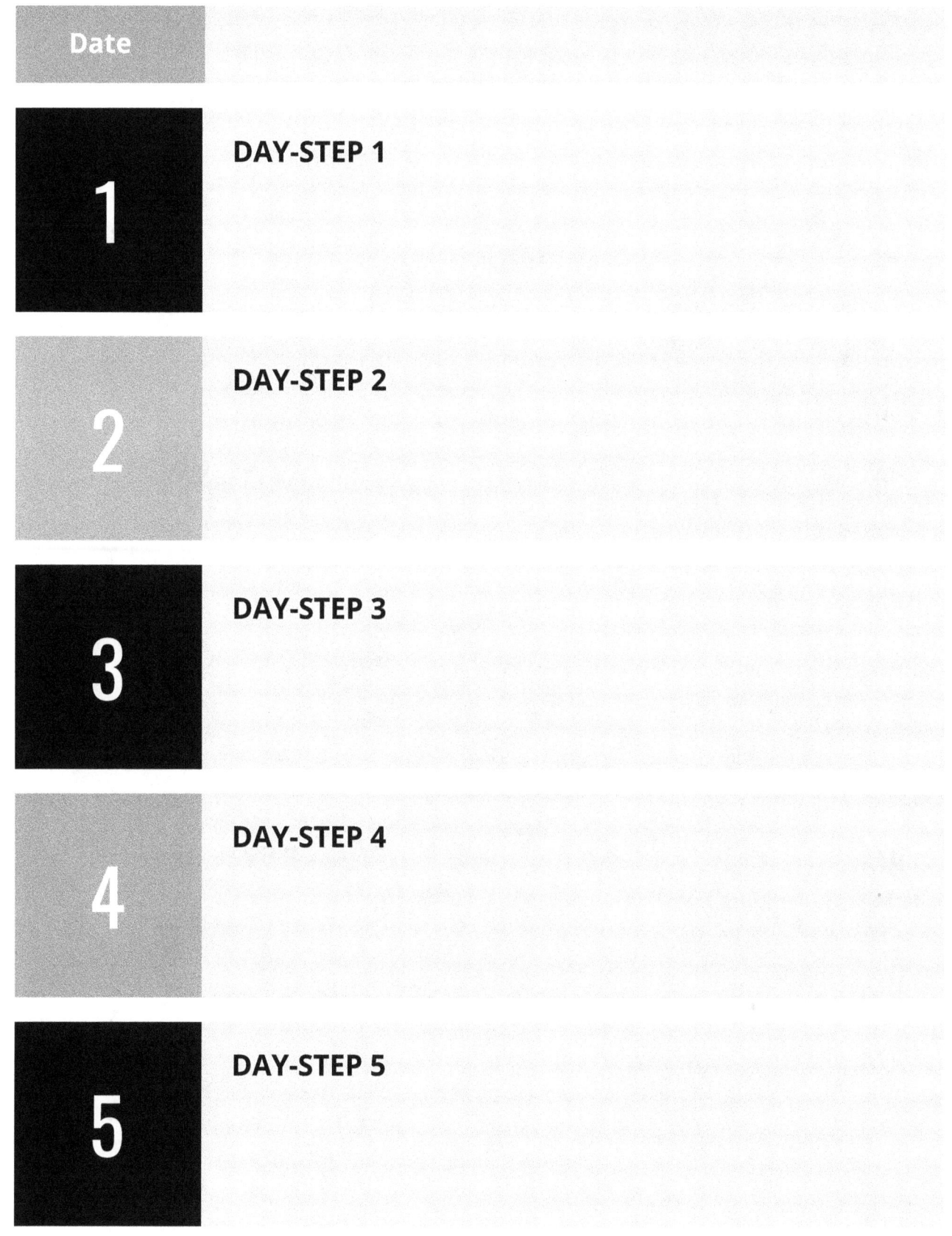

DAILY PLANNER

Date

6 AM

7 AM

8 AM

9 AM

10 AM

11 AM

12 PM

1 PM

2 PM

3 PM

4 PM

5 PM

6 PM

7 PM

8 PM

9 PM

10 PM

PRIORITIES

NOTES

REVIEW

WEEKLY PLANNER

Weekly goals

MONDAY

TUESDAY

WEDNESDAY

THURSDAY

FRIDAY

SATURDAY

SUNDAY

PRIORITIES

NOTES

REVIEW

90-DAY PLANNER

Long-term goal

Divide long-term goals into smaller, more doable short-term ones.

Prepare your goals based on your mission, vision, or purpose.

MONTH 1	MONTH 2	MONTH 3

www.peachesandcream.org

Do not forget to purchase the **Support Your Mental (SYM) "Planner and Workbook"** to learn more about yourself and practice exercises that can help you cope with your mental challenges. The planner and workbook also provide you with guidance and support.

The Certificate of Completion is on the next page. Once you have completed the "Support Your Mental" book, sign your name on the certificate, print it, and frame it. **Cruise over to the certificate.**

CERTIFICATE

OF PARTICIPATION
COMPLETION

This Certificate Presented to :

has successfully completed the Support Your Mental Book and has learned valuable insights and skills to enhance their mental well-being. Presented by Peaches and Cream Foundation.

Ella Butcher
Founder

Lateshia Butcher
Chairwoman

www.ingramcontent.com/pod-product-compliance
Lightning Source LLC
Chambersburg PA
CBHW081459040426
42446CB00016B/3313